THE
AWAKENING
IN
WALES

THE

AWAKENING

IN

WALES

JESSIE PENN-LEWIS

WHITAKER
HOUSE

Unless otherwise indicated, all Scripture quotations are taken from the Revised Version of the Holy Bible. Scripture quotations marked (KJV) are taken from the King James Version of the Holy Bible. The Scripture quotation marked (WEY) is taken from *The New Testament in Modern Speech: An Idiomatic Translation into Everyday English from the Text of "The Resultant Greek Testament"* by R. F. (Richard Francis) Weymouth.

Boldface type in the Scripture quotations indicates the author's emphasis.

THE AWAKENING IN WALES

(Previously published as *The Awakening in Wales and Some of the Hidden Springs*)

ISBN: 978-1-60374-968-8
eBook ISBN: 978-1-60374-252-8
Printed in the United States of America
© 1905, 2014 by Whitaker House

Whitaker House
1030 Hunt Valley Circle
New Kensington, PA 15068
www.whitakerhouse.com

Library of Congress Cataloging-in-Publication Data (Pending)

1 2 3 4 5 6 7 8 9 10 11 ⨈ 21 20 19 18 17 16 15 14

CONTENTS

PREFACE

In the days of the primitive church, it was considered necessary that a full and authentic record should be written concerning the coming of the Holy Spirit, and all the mighty workings that followed His descent into the upper room at Jerusalem.

When the right time comes, such a treatise concerning the outpouring of the Holy Spirit in Wales in 1904–1905 will be found necessary, for Wales is "making history"—divine history—these days. Doubtless, also, the Lord Himself is preparing a "Luke" for this service!

In view, then, of future history, it becomes the binding duty of each one with authentic information to contribute his or her quota to the common fund. Such a duty lies on me because I have, for the past few years, been on the watchtower, watching the movements of God, and I may not withhold from the church of God what my eyes have seen of His mighty works, preparing and leading up to this awakening, which we trust and pray may be the beginning of the wider fulfillment of the prophecy of Joel.

The greater part of all that I have written in the following pages is from firsthand information, which has come to me in such a way that I could not fail to see the Lord directing it to me for the purpose of this story. And I am greatly indebted to the clergy, ministers, and others who have sent me various accounts of the work, and who have, in some instances, translated it from Welsh to English—demanding no little labor and time in the midst of other pressing claims. I have thought it best to omit all these names, with the exception of those already publicly connected with the revival, although I recognize that in the days of Pentecost, the story was told in all its simplicity of truth—with no thought of honor to the instruments of God as *"they rehearsed all things that God had done with them"* (Acts 14:27).

To obtain a wide vision, I have also sought to write from the viewpoint of the Mount of God. The spouse in Canticles cries to the sister-bride, *"Come with me from Lebanon, my bride...look from the top"* (Song of Solomon 4:8). May we heed His call and *"ascend into the hill of the LORD"* (Psalm 24:3) and *"stand in his holy place"* (verse 3), from where we may watch in the world "the voice of the Lord hewing out flames of fire" (see Psalm 29:7) and "breaking the cedars" (see verse 5). But it is obvious that the following pages cannot possibly unfold all that the Lord has wrought in the prayer movement or His inner workings in the Principality of Wales.[1] Indeed, the story of His marvelous workings in each of the few centers I have briefly referred to would easily fill a chapter.

I have recorded only what I know of some of those springs of the revival—springs that were, up to that time, unseen by the world. I do this not only for the sake of future history, but because it is of the most vital importance that the people of God discern the true inwardness of God's workings, lest they be occupied with the outward manifestations and seek to copy what can only be produced by God Himself, when His people obey the conditions of blessing. With this special object in view, I have chosen, out of the quantity of material in my hands, to record those instances of the working of God which emphasize the aspect I have enlarged upon in chapters 5 and 6—i.e., that God works from the midst of a Spirit-filled people out upon the world. If the "revival dawn" in Wales to increase to noonday power, all who long for worldwide revival must see to it that they hasten the day by personally entering the Spirit-filled life, while congregations must seek to have their "Pentecost"—what may never have entered their minds before as possible.

In closing, I cannot refrain from mentioning the "romantic coincidence" that has come to me personally within the last year in the

1. The Principality of Wales spanned from 1216–1536.

renewal of my childhood friendship with Dr. Cynddylan Jones. As a girl of fourteen, I was the little companion of Dr. Jones and my father, who together were convalescents in a hydropathic establishment near Bath after serious illness. My father was taken to the heavenly home, and Dr. Jones was left to continue his ministry for God, little dreaming that the child who played around him in those days would, in later years, have the privilege and joy of linking service with him and telling the story of the great revival in their native land!

May the eternal Spirit use these messages toward the fulfilling of His desire to lead the church of God back to Calvary and to Pentecost. Then *"the glory of the LORD shall be revealed, and all flesh shall see it together: for the mouth of the LORD hath spoken it"* (Isaiah 40:5).

—Jessie Penn-Lewis

INTRODUCTION

Wales is a land of periodic revivals. In the middle of the eighteenth century, *"a live coal...from off the altar"* (Isaiah 6:6) touched the lips of Daniel Rowlands, a clergyman of the Church of England, and inspired him with a fervor that no opposition could quench. The polite and respectable Christians of the period called him the "cracked clergyman" of Llangeitho. But if he were cracked, the Welsh nation has reason to be forever grateful, for through the "cracks," he beheld God and eternity, and a vision filled his soul with boundless enthusiasm.

In a few years, all of Wales was ablaze. People from far and near came to witness the stirring effects of his preaching; the hearers wept and shouted, thus outraging all the proprieties. Did that marvelous revival leave anything behind of permanent value to the nation? Yes. First, just as the revival in England left behind a new religious communion, the great Wesleyan Methodist Church, so in Wales the revival created a new denomination, the Calvinistic Methodist Church, which in numbers, influence, and in learning, ranks with the foremost of the denominations in the country. Second, it gave Wales its hymnology. Till then, the nation had no hymns. Now we have a heritage of hymns rich beyond compare. These hymns revitalized the religious life, and as a consequence, the nation has moved on a higher level ever since.

In course of time, that movement expended its force. But in the beginning of the last century, another revival started. John Elias with his theological sermons, Christmas Evans with his poetical sermons, and Williams of Wern with his philosophical sermons, traveled the country, proclaiming the doctrines of grace, each in his own way, and overpowering their hearers, throwing them into a religious ecstasy. And, once again, the large congregation shouted and sang with joy. All of Wales was like a boiling cauldron. Gradually, the flames of emotion died out. What was left—ashes? By no means; that convulsion in the spiritual experience of the population raised the national life to a higher level. Emotionalism? Always; but it fed the roots of intellect and infused new life into the Tree of Knowledge, as well as the Tree of Life.

However it be among other nations, in Wales, the life is always the light. As the first revival gave us our hymnology, so the second revival gave us our theology. There probably were not men learned enough to write standard books of their own, but there were many who were able to translate the standard works of other authors. Accordingly, under the influence of this revival, great books were rendered into the vernacular of Wales: *The Person of Christ, Justification,* and *The Work of the Holy Spirit* by Dr. Owen; *Matthew Henry's Commentary*; and a number of other Puritan books. Under its influence, Bunyan's pilgrim learned to speak Welsh on his journey to the Celestial City! In the absence of light literature, the farmers and the peasantry spent their long winter evenings pondering over these books, discussing their teaching in their adult Sunday schools and in their weekday evening meetings and becoming thoroughly grounded in the fundamental doctrines of salvation. Puritanism entered the blood of the Welshman; it still colors his every thought and can never be expelled. Hence his aversion to rites and ceremonies—to all appeals to his aesthetic nature—and his readiness, on the other hand, to respond to all appeals to his spiritual nature.

In 1850, the enthusiasm of the former days had died out. Church life was placid, even to torpidity. The elderly men and women were calling to mind the years of the right hand of the Almighty and sighing for a wee bit of a breeze. And in 1859, the third revival broke out. Humphrey Jones, a young Wesleyan minister, catching the fire of the American revival, crossed the ocean to convey the flame to his native land. He held prayer and preaching meetings; and all of the people from the countryside in North Cardigan were talking about the young revivalist. Alas! His bodily frame could not stand the strain, and in three or four months, his nervous system broke down, and he never faced a congregation again.

But he had not labored in vain, for before his collapse, he had imparted the fire to a neighbor of his, the Reverend David Morgan, a Calvinistic Methodist minister and a man of splendid physique. The transformation worked in the latter was simply miraculous. I know that which I speak, for I was an eyewitness of it all. He toured the country from Holyhead to Cardiff, spoke as one inspired, and towered high above all his compeers during the three years of his strange uplifting. Crowds hung upon the words of his lips; the ungodly cried out in agony of soul; and the saints shouted for joy—their noise like the noise of many waters. All the country was aflame. It is computed that about one hundred thousand converts were added to the churches.

There were more critics and scoffers then than there are now.

If therefore the whole church be assembled together, and all speak…, and there come in men unlearned or unbelieving, will they not say that ye are mad?   (1 Corinthians 14:23)

Literally, will they not say that you are under the influence of a demon? That was probably the criticism of unbelievers on the revival in Corinth; that certainly was their criticism on the revival of 1859 in Wales! Fortunately, there were others who were more sensitive to spiritual influences, and who replied, "Well, well, if this be the work of the devil, he must be a very new devil to Wales. The old one sent the people to the bars; the new sends them to the churches. The old made them dance and swear; the new makes them leap and praise."

"By their fruits ye shall know them."   (Matthew 7:20)

Emotionalism, extravagance—yes; but they burnt out the old impurities. Wales was lifted high on the crest of that revival wave; and when the wave subsided, what was left—froth? No, but higher aspirations after holiness and an intense love of learning. Since then, the number of worshipping places has doubled, thousands of schools have been built, and three national colleges have been established— all having their roots in the revivification of the religious life of nearly fifty years ago. The first revival gave us our hymnology, the second our theology, and the third our educational system, which competent authorities pronounce to be second to none in the world today. Like the overflowing of the Nile, every revival leaves a rich deposit behind to fertilize the national character.

That memorable revival in the roll of the years spent its force. For the last ten years, the spiritual life in our churches has been becoming more and more depressed. Our best spirits were lamenting the impending lapse of our fatherland into barbarism. Earnest crying was made unto heaven. For months, we felt that there was a vague, indefinite, mysterious something in the air—a going in the top of the mulberry trees. The godly mothers and maidens were the first to feel the return of the tide, which for the last few months has swept all before it. The story of this fourth revival will be told in the following pages by one in complete sympathy with all spiritual movements, and who possesses the advantage of thoroughly understanding the generous impulses of the Celtic heart and the subtle windings of the Celtic brain. But I may be allowed to indicate two or three of its outstanding features:

1. It is independent of all human organizations—straight from heaven. Missions are not *revivals*. Men can organize the former, not the latter, and it is a pity that the distinction is so often overlooked. Man's method of saving the world is by costly and complicated machinery—salvation by mechanics; but God's method is by vital energy—salvation by dynamics. Saint Paul said, *"I am not ashamed of the gospel: for it is the power of God unto salvation"* (Romans 1:16). Paul, the missionary, relying upon prayer and the dynamic power of the gospel, changed the face of the Roman Empire. And in Wales today, all is spontaneous. The dynamite is working; explosion follows explosion. And already, scores of thousands of rough, hard stones have been loosened from the quarry of corrupt humanity, and whole explosions frequently and powerfully take place. Should people wonder why there is tumult and confusion? Better is the confusion of the city than the order of the cemetery.

2. Much importance is attached to the work of the Spirit, at least in its initial stages. Up to this time, the work of Christ has been the all-important truth, to the exclusion of the doctrine the Spirit. Much emphasis has been put on receiving Christ, scant stress on receiving the Spirit. Now, however, the question is coming to the forefront, *"Did ye receive the Holy Ghost when ye believed?"* (Acts 19:2). There were thousands of believers in our churches who had, like the disciples Saint Paul met at Ephesus, received Christ but had never received the Holy Spirit. The mark of Christ's blood was upon them, but where was the mark of the Spirit's anointing? Saved themselves, they made no attempt to save others. The present revival, however, while not obscuring the doctrine of the cross, has brought into prominence the doctrine of the Spirit. Thousands of Christians who had received the Christ have now received the Holy Spirit, and as a consequence, they are filled with the Spirit of service—no task seems to them too hard for Christ's sake.

While this doctrine is by no means new theology, it has assumed in the present movement a new form, at least in experience. Orthodoxy has always conceded that conscience speaks within us; but in practice, we have effected too wide a separation between conscience and the Holy Spirit. This revival has again united these two. The man says, "Something tells me to do this and avoid that." The young revivalist says, "Something tells me to do this or that." Why don't you be honest? Why don't you say "some *One*"? And the revivalist is right. A thing can never speak. It is not something but some One who speaks, and it is none other than the third Person of the Holy Trinity. Does this not invest conscience with grand sacredness? We all believe in the need of the Spirit to regenerate and sanctify, to accomplish the great tasks of life, including the works that we know no human power can affect. But alas, we are not in the habit of introducing the Spirit into the common acts of our everyday life. But the Scripture teaches us to seek the Spirit's guidance in all things—He is the source of all prudence and wisdom.

3. The third feature is enthusiasm, a feature common to all revivals. Many Christians who love gentility and moderation would like to receive the baptism of the Spirit without the baptism of fire. But what

God has joined cannot be sundered. John the Baptist said of Christ, *"He shall baptize you with the Holy Ghost and with fire"* (Matthew 3:11). Here is the verse—now what will you do with it? In the original text, there is only one preposition in this verse—one *"with"* instead of two "withs"—to show the identity of the two baptisms—or, rather, that there is but one baptism. Wherever the Spirit descends, He brings fire in His train.

> *There appeared unto them tongues parting asunder, like as of fire; and it sat upon each one of them. And they were all filled with the Holy Spirit, and began to speak with other tongues, as the Spirit gave them utterance.*　　　　　(Acts 2:3–4)

Hearts of fire and tongues of flame. Is enthusiasm permissible in every department of life but forbidden in church life? A thousand times, No. How does the apostle speak about it? *"Fervent in spirit; serving the Lord"* (Romans 12:11). The word *fervent* literally means "boiling." So we should be "boiling in spirit." Let no one be ashamed of "boiling" in their service to the Savior. At all events, I prefer the congregations that boil over to the congregations that do not boil at all. *"The effectual fervent prayer of a righteous man availeth much"* (James 5:16 KJV). Literally, this means "the boiling prayer." The cold prayer of a good man will avail nothing in heaven or on earth; but the boiling prayer of a righteous man has performed wonders before now and will perform them again.

How very cold and formal the prayers of the church have been for many long years! But for the last four months, there has been everywhere a marked change—the prayers have been boiling and whole multitudes have been thrown into a state of extraordinary fervor. It rejoices me to see the rising generation boil with a great enthusiasm in service to the Christ—the mark of the "boiling" will be on them as long as they live. After boiling, none of them are the same as they were before. Hundreds of our young men and women have been brought up religiously in the home and in the church; but their religion has been cold, formal, and following a routine. Hardly any of them have the courage to bow in public prayer, with the knowledge that only aged men engage publicly in the weekly prayer meetings.

Behold the difference! Now our young people flock to the services; prayers flow spontaneously from their lips like water from the spring; praise ascends to heaven like the carol of birds in spring. No forcing, no inviting—spontaneity characterizes the proceedings from beginning to end. No one is ashamed of confessing Christ as his or her Savior; rather, the shame is on the other side. All the chapels are crowded; the valleys and mountains ring with praise. The following story will show how gamblers refuse money won in bets before their conversion, how prizefighters are now soulwinners, how thieves restore stolen goods, how husbands return to their deserted homes, and how enemies turn into friends. Scores of pages can be filled with the striking conversions that took place in the Christian church.

Do we justify the extravagances? Not more than Paul justified them in Corinth! (See 1 Corinthians 14.) We know what they mean, for we are able to interpret the tongues. Out of the confusion will emerge order and beauty and life. All criticisms are met by the prophet's question, *"What is the chaff to the wheat?"* (Jeremiah 23:28 KJV).

—*Dr. J. Cynddylan Jones*

DYMA GARIAD[2]

"Here Is Love"

Here is Love, vast as the ocean,
Lovingkindness as the flood,
When the Prince of Life our ransom
Shed for us His precious blood;

Who His love will not remember?
Who can cease to sing His praise?
He can never be forgotten
Through Heaven's everlasting days.

On the Mount of Crucifixion
Fountains opened deep and wide;
Through the floodgates of God's mercy
Flowed a vast and gracious tide;

Grace and love, like mighty rivers,
Poured incessant from above.
And Heaven's peace and perfect justice
Kissed a guilty world in love.

---

2. The "Love Song" of the revival. English rendering by Principal Edwards, Cardiff.

ONE

THE ORIGIN OF THE PRAYER MOVEMENT

After the tragedy at Calvary, and the glorious resurrection and ascension of Him who is now alive forevermore, the ascended Lord sat down at the right hand of the Majesty on High. As the fruit of His cross and passion, He received of the Father the *"promise of the Holy Ghost"* (Acts 2:33) for His redeemed ones. He then poured Him forth upon the company of men and women gathered together in one accord at the upper room in Jerusalem—the city where He was crucified. Some of Jesus' last words to His disciples before He ascended had been, *"I send forth the promise of my Father upon you: but tarry ye in the city, until ye be clothed with power from on high"* (Luke 24:49). Returning from Mount Olive to Jerusalem, His disciples set themselves to obey and in one accord, they continued steadfastly in prayer until at last the day dawned, and the Holy Spirit came as the rushing of a mighty breath.

The word used to describe the Holy Spirit's advent is significant. The Lord Jesus spoke of the breath of the Spirit to Nicodemus when He told him that men who were dead in sin must have a new birth—a birth from above, which would come by the breathing of the Spirit of life upon them, so that they are begotten of God. (See John 3:7.) And *"the wind bloweth where it listeth"* (John 3:8 KJV)! Men could hear and see the effects of the wind but did not know *"whence it cometh, and whither it goeth"* (John 3:8).

Later on, we read that on the first Easter day, the risen Lord stood in the midst of His disciples, and, showing them His hands and His side, scarred with the marks of Calvary, He breathed on them, saying, "*Receive ye the Holy Ghost*" (John 20:22) or, as the *Wycliffe Bible* has it, "*Take ye the Holy Ghost.*"

We cannot doubt that the disciples received the Holy Spirit when the risen Lord breathed upon them. But their immediate afterlife shows that it was not the energizing for service and the clothing with divine power that they received, for the Lord so expressly bade them tarry for these things before they attempted witnessing for Him. The breathing of the Holy Spirit upon them on the first Easter day seems to have been the preparation for receiving the Pentecostal fullness of the divine Spirit. They would have sorely failed to enter into His greater purposes for them had they said, "But we received the Holy Spirit on the day of His resurrection," not waiting in Jerusalem until they were baptized in the Holy Spirit, or clothed with Him, as the Lord had promised.

But they obeyed and tarried, possibly not even knowing what the outcome would be, until "*suddenly there came from heaven a sound as of the rushing of a mighty breath*" (Acts 2:2). The breath of God, which gives new birth to every believer, now came forth with such force and volume that it filled the very atmosphere of the house where they were sitting. The believers were now, so to speak, submerged in the Holy Spirit, as well as indwelt by Him. In this intensely surcharged atmosphere, the divine Spirit became manifest—apparently to sight as well as hearing—"*and there appeared unto them tongues parting asunder, like as of fire* ["*distributing themselves*" (wey)]" (Acts 2:3) and resting upon each one present, until each of them—no matter their temperament, education, training, position, sex, or age—"*began to speak…as the Spirit gave them utterance*" (verse 4).

The city of Jerusalem knew nothing of the little company quietly meeting and praying in the upper room! But now they could not be hid. Hearing the sound of voices, the multitude came together and saw the Spirit-filled company so manifestly under the control of some power which lifted them out of themselves that some said, "*These men are full of new wine*" (Acts 2:13 kjv), while others were amazed and marveled, saying, "*Are not all these which speak Galilæans*" (Acts 2:7), who were untaught, uncultured people from the province of Galilee?

The world had been going on its way, ignorant of all that God was silently working in the spiritual realm to bring about the purpose of the ages. But now, the gathering multitude cried, "*What meaneth this?*" (Acts 2:12). Ah, momentous things had happened in the unseen realm, and all that had been worked by the death of the God-man at Calvary was now made manifest to the world that crucified Him! The third Person of the Godhead, the eternal Spirit of the Father, came forth to bear witness to the crucified and risen Lord and to clothe human beings with divine authority as His messengers.

In answer to the charge of being filled with wine, Peter—the very man who, just a fortnight before, had denied his Lord in that same city—rose to speak. Speaking under the constraint of the divine Spirit, he said,

> *This is that which was spoken by the prophet Joel; and it shall come to pass in the last days, saith God, I will pour out of my Spirit upon all flesh: and your sons and your daughters shall prophesy…on my servants and on my handmaidens I will pour out in those days of my Spirit; and they shall prophesy.*
>
> (Acts 2:16–18)

Let us mark the words, for they vitally concern the people of God today. "*This is that which was spoken by the prophet Joel*" (Acts 2:16), said the apostle; not "this is the entire fulfillment of the prophecy." It is written, "*I will pour out of my Spirit upon all flesh*" (Acts 2:17). This speaks of a larger circle than one hundred twenty men and women; yea, an even larger circle than the three thousand and five thousand souls. "*And believers were the more added to the Lord, multitudes both of men and women*" (Acts 5:14). This prophecy undoubtedly foretells a much wider fulfillment, with many more people than those who received the Holy Spirit at Pentecost.

Christ said, "*In those days will I pour out my spirit*" (Joel 2:29). "[The expression of this verse] is in the long Hebrew tense, expressing continuance of action, literally an incoming, unfinished, and continuous outpouring," says Dr. Woods Smythe. It therefore appears that the words *"in those days"* cover the whole dispensation of the Spirit, beginning with the day of Pentecost. The purpose of God was manifestly a beginning in the upper room; and a continuing upon wider and wider circles as the overflowing stream of life reached *"the uttermost part of the earth"* (Acts 1:8); but, alas, the church, instead of abiding in a Pentecostal condition, drifted further and further away from it. Nevertheless, the Word of God stands sure. The church will be brought back to her Pentecost, when she knows her need and turns to the Lord.

The Fulfillment of Joel's Prophecy in Wales

In the prophecy of Joel, we see the work of the Holy Spirit foreshadowed under the figure of rain. Joel speaks of the Lord's response to the cry of His people, when He would cause to come down for them the *"former rain"* and the *"latter rain"* (Joel 2:23). Then afterward should come the outpouring of the Spirit upon all flesh and a time of such manifestly supernatural workings of the Spirit, *"that whosoever shall call on the name of the LORD shall be delivered"* (Joel 2:32). The *"former rain"* was always given in Palestine to germinate and to mature the sown seed. The *"latter rain"* was essential to the plumping out of the grain for its ripening and fitting for the harvest. How clear is the forecast of God's purposes toward His people in the gifts of the Holy Spirit.

We need not now attempt to trace the divine movements in the world preceding the first Pentecost. Were we to do so, we should find them strikingly parallel to those in recent years, when the condition of the professing Christian church has become similar to the Jewish church at the close of the dispensation before the Messiah appeared.

It is sufficient for us to emphasize that Joel's prophecy clearly sets forth the preparation of the people of God by seeking Him in prayer. We read that they are brought by His providential dealings to a consciousness of their need and are summoned to leave all their interests, seeking His face in one accord. Then would come the Lord's response in overflow of personal blessing, and the pouring out of His Spirit in such measure that the world would be touched and the sinners moved to call upon the Lord.

Indeed, the first Pentecost at Jerusalem exactly fulfilled this forecast. Bereft of the One who had been with them in bodily presence as Teacher and Guide; faced with His command to go forth and disciple all nations; conscious of their powerlessness to fulfill this commission, and their lack of position, culture, knowledge, and all the resources that would command the attention of the world to their message, the little company of disciples gathered in one accord to pray until they were equipped with power from on high.

Prayer preceded the first Pentecost, and prayer must precede the wider outpouring of the Spirit in the last days. Therefore, the true members of Christ all over the world must be drawn by the Spirit within them into one accord as they ask God to pour forth His Spirit according to His Word. The extent of the one will govern the extent of the other, for prayer prepares the channels for the Holy Spirit to fill and flow out into the world.

The question therefore arises as to whether there has been in recent years any indication of the special preparation of the church for the wider fulfillment of Joel's prophecy. If we find this to be so, our faith will be strengthened, and our vision cleared, to see that the revival in Wales may be the beginning of the latter rain which will prepare the church of God for the Lord's appearing and draw into the kingdom all who will to be saved.

To obtain a wide vision, let us in heart and mind now ascend into the secret place of the Most High, having boldness to enter the holiest place by the blood of Jesus, and look out with Him upon the world, watching the movements of His Spirit among His people. We may only find the veil lifted here and there and obtain but glimpses into His workings, but these will suffice to give insight into His preparations over the earth for the fulfillment of His purposes toward men.

The Prayer Movement

We will go in thought back to the year 1898 or 1899 and, glancing into an institute in America, see gathered there three to four hundred children of God, meeting every Saturday night to pray for a worldwide revival. In this institute, we find men and women from every clime seeking equipment for the preaching of the gospel. Their hearts yearned over their own lands, and the blessing that they sought was worldwide. After a time, a few began to stay in prayer late at night and ceased not until the early hours of the Sabbath morning. Among them was their leader. Conscious that they who pray must be ready to be instrumental in answering their own prayers, they offered themselves to God for any special service in the bringing about of the prayed-for revival.

Rapidly, we cross in vision to another faraway land; in Australia, there was a band of ministers and laymen who had met for eleven whole years every Saturday afternoon, pleading with God for a big revival. In a wondrous chain of divine workings, we next see a messenger called out from the heart of the praying company in America—the very one who had laid himself at the feet of the Lord of the harvest, ready for all His commands—who would work as God's instrument in Australia and be an answer to their prayers.

In 1901, we look into the great city of Melbourne and see fifty missioners holding services in fifty different centers of the city, while forty thousand praying souls met in two thousand homes for prayer meetings, encircling the city with prayer. Many met for half-nights of prayer, and Melbourne was moved from end to end by the mighty workings of the Spirit of God.

The Prayer Circles

We come again in swift thought back to Great Britain, and look in at the huge meetings of five thousand Christians gathered at Keswick in July 1902. Hark! The story of the home prayer circles in Melbourne was told among those who were gathered. The hearts of workers were burdened and sad. Weary of organization and effort, they were not impressed by mere prayer unions. But quickly, the spark from the fire in Australia fell into many hearts. Home prayer circles began to form— the "twos and threes" of those who were truly burdened for worldwide revival! Ah, this is the call of God! If this city was thus girdled with prayer, why not the world? Quickly, the names of those who were drawn by God to pray were sent in from all parts of the earth, until thousands of praying hearts were circling the globe in prayer. It was God's prayer union gathered and guided by Him, with no organization, no membership fee, and no staff—just the few who registered the names as a labor of love for souls. And their prayer was now for the outpouring of the Spirit; in other words, for a Pentecost in the church of God.

Just one month earlier, in faraway India, the divine Spirit had laid the same burden upon the servants of God and had guided them—without any conscious connection with the prayer movement in other lands—to form a prayer circle of those who would unite to plead for an outpouring of the Spirit upon that dark and needy land. Manifestly, the Spirit of God had been simultaneously moving the people of God in various parts of the world to pray for the same thing, creating the cry for that which He was preparing to do.

Later, in the year 1902, when the circles of prayer were formed, the praying people of God—undoubtedly including many prayer groups and praying hearts that were not visibly linked with the world-wide circles—united in one accord to ask for the promised Pentecost.

It is also significant that in this year, a pamphlet entitled *A Revival Call to the Churches* was issued, and it obtained a wide circulation. Another pamphlet called *Back to Pentecost* was issued the same year, showing how God led the thoughts of His people and prepared them for His purposes of grace.

Can we discern any immediate effects of the world-girdling prayer? Within a year, there began to be signs of awakening in various quarters, and *"the voice of the* Lord *[was] upon the waters"* (Psalm 29:3). But there was not yet any movement of the Spirit, which would reveal to the eyes of the world the characteristics of Pentecost.

As in the days of Anna and Simeon, there were many hidden souls in the secret of God's counsels. One such soul was present in Keswick at the time of the call to prayer. This woman had offered herself to

God some two years before this event for the special service of intercession, and the story of His dealings is best told in her own words:

I had read words to this effect, "If even one life could be fully surrendered to God to use as He wanted for prayer, most wonderful results would follow—and He needs such an one." Then I knelt down, and very humbly told Him if He would take me and use me for prayer, I would be willing. When I said fully from my heart, "Yes, Lord," it seemed as if a hand was placed on me pressing me lower and lower, until I had no life left in me—and I wept.

For some months, I was used for prayer in small things, but one day about six months later, all was utter darkness. As usual, I went to Him, but the darkness continued for about a week. Then one morning, about ten o'clock, the agony became terrible, and I cried, "Lord, what is it?" He answered, "Come with Me, and I will show you the sin in this place."

We seemed to go into all the worst parts of the district, and I saw sin as never before. I cried out for the people. The prayer was, "O Lord, send a revival into this place." Then came perfect peace until the next morning at the same time, when the Lord called me again and took me further afield. The same thing happened for a whole week until I was agonizing for a worldwide revival, as He took me into places where the gospel had never been heard. Then all this ceased.

From this time, I was watching for the revival and wondering how the Lord would send it. When we heard of any special one being used, I went to the Lord and said, "Is this Thine instrument, Lord?" And He answered, "Only one, Child." Again, I went about another much-used soul, and the same answer came, with this addition, *I have something more than this.*

At Keswick in 1902—the first I had ever attended—prayer circles were announced for a worldwide revival. Then, I went to the Lord and cried, "Lord, why must they pray for what

Thou hast already promised?" Then He said, "This revival is an accomplished fact in My kingdom." And I said, "Why does it not come, Lord, without these prayer circles?" He replied, "I am ready, but My children are not. Before it comes, they must preach the word of the cross—the message of Calvary."

The phrase "I am ready, but My children are not" shows that the worldwide circles of prayer were mainly necessary for the purpose of creating desire among the people of God and preparing the channels for the coming rain. The phrase "they must preach the cross" also tells us that God Himself cannot send revival until the gospel of Calvary is proclaimed.

But in one accord, the people's cry has ascended to heaven. Christ upon His throne is ready to bless. The blood of the Son of God which has been *"trodden under foot"* (Hebrews 10:29) and counted *"an unholy thing"* (verse 29) will be borne witness to from heaven.

The Renewed Preaching of the Cross

Where will we now turn our eyes to see His workings? Can we perceive a marked renewal of the preaching of the cross? Yes, certainly. Early in 1903, the records in the papers showed on every side that the messengers of God were being led by Him to proclaim afresh the message of Calvary. At annual meetings, opening services, and special conferences, the keynote again and again was the "need for direct preaching of the cross," while a well-known religious paper remarked that there were "welcome signs of reversal to the old gospel of Calvary."

In light of all this, it is significant to find that at the Keswick Convention of 1903, when the windows of heaven were opened and the Holy Spirit swept as an overflowing stream over the huge gatherings of five thousand men and women—many of them from distant parts of the earth who sought the power of the Holy Spirit—unveiling to them in fresh and vivid power the cross of Calvary. Almost every servant of God entrusted with His messages proclaimed in one accord *"the word of the cross"* (1 Corinthians 1:18) as the power of God to save from bondage and the guilt of sin, and being *"crucified with Christ"* (Galatians 2:16) as the secret of deliverance.

The writer heard Christians of long-standing declare they had never before realized how awful and humiliating was the death of Christ. Two great truths were set forth among us: first, that Christ died for us; second, that we are identified with Him in death. To thousands of Christians the second point was an aspect of the work of Christ that hitherto had escaped their notice. Here was the secret of rest and power presented in a word.[3]

In 1902, the Holy Spirit had drawn His people to pray for a worldwide revival; and in 1903, the eternal Spirit broke forth upon the people of God gathered from the ends of the earth and led them back to Calvary.

Moreover, in 1903, the Spirit of God unveiled to one of His honored servants in faraway India the cross of Calvary in new and vivid power, revealing to him that for forty years He had been preparing him for the work of sending forth the word of the cross to every tongue and tribe and nation in millions of booklets containing the full-orbed message of Calvary.

Yes, prayer must truly prepare God's people for the moving of the Spirit in Pentecostal power; and when the Holy Spirit comes forth, He bears witness to Calvary, as in the day of the first Pentecost in Jerusalem.

"O! ANFON DI YR YSBRYD GLAN"

O! send Thy Holy Spirit, Lord,
In Jesus' blessed name,
O! let Thy Spirit now descend
In tongues of sacred flame!
According to Thy promise, Lord,
Shed freely from above
The Holy Spirit in His strength
To manifest Thy love.
A sound of abundance of rain.

---

3. S. A. McC., *The Life of Faith.*

TWO

THE PROPHET OF THE REVIVAL IN WALES

"There is the sound of abundance of rain."
—1 Kings 18:41

But where in these days can be found the conditions necessary for the mighty working of God? It must be, and can only be, where the atonement of Christ is proclaimed and where the Scriptures are accepted sincerely as the Word of the living God.

We look toward the little principality of Wales and find these conditions there. Speaking generally, the pulpit has been true to the evangelical faith in all its essentials, and the gospel of the grace of God has been faithfully preached to the people. The nation as a whole has clung to the faith of their fathers—the exception being the few who have been touched by the spirit of criticism and unbelief so prevalent in other lands. True, the people may have been living upon the traditions of the past, yet there has not been a departure from *"the faith which was once for all delivered unto the saints"* (Jude 1:3).

Wales has also had special advantages in its Sunday schools, where people of all ages gathered to learn the Word of God and earnest efforts were directed to make the teaching effectual by systematic study and Scripture examinations. Then, again, we find the congregational festivals for singing and placing the words of hymns full of the message of Calvary into the people's memories. Groups of churches would practice the same selection of hymns through the winter, and then a day would be set apart for a festival under the conductorship of a leading musical teacher. In conducting one of these festivals, the late Joseph Parry, musician and doctor, said that the coming revival would be a singing one. With the gospel of Calvary in their minds and the hymns about Calvary in their memories, the nation needed the breath of God to quicken their traditional faith into living power.

The all-wise God looks forth upon the world and finds here in this little country the conditions necessary for the breaking forth of His Spirit in Pentecostal power. Let us see whether there are traces of the prayer movement in the principality. We do not know whether the story of the world-girdling prayer circles reached many in Wales, but we find the Holy Spirit creating in individuals, and groups of twos and threes, the very same cry He was calling forth all over the world.

In 1901, the Lord drew near to one of His servants in the ministry and gave him such a revelation of His glory that be cried, as did Isaiah, *"Woe is me!"* (Isaiah 6:5), and he entered into a life in God he had not known before. Then, burdened over the spiritual condition of the country, he spent hours in prayer in a quiet spot on the banks of a Welsh river, pleading with God with many tears that He would come forth in power and work in the land.

Again, in a quiet town in the western part of Wales, we hear of two and three women meeting together for prayer over the course of several years, pleading for revival among the women of the town.

Then we go to the Rhondda Valley, where the Spirit of God swept with great power. Here were some who had been pleading for years for a revival that would "sweep over the whole world." These souls were taken in to the secrets of God, and the Holy Spirit said to one of them just three days before the valley was moved by the mighty tide of life, *"Get thee up...there is the sound of abundance of rain"* (1 Kings 18:41).

In Monmouthshire, the hand of the Lord was upon two sisters, (one an invalid) who, between the years 1903–1904, were burdened over the prevalence of sin and the increase of crime in the county. One sister said tearfully, "I cannot sleep day nor night because my dear Lord is despised and set at naught."

Another child of God—a retiring, timid lady—bemoaning the deadness of the churches, said, "I will die unless God exerts His power and sends a revival!"

We hear of three ministers of the gospel meeting together in May 1903 for prayer and conference and who were drawn together by a sense of need. They were utterly dissatisfied with their own Christian experience and distressed at the condition of their churches, because worldliness and apathy was among their officers and members. Once again, it was a group of three! They decided to form a prayer circle and resolved to meet at ten o'clock each morning to pray for one another and their churches. This prayer group throws light upon the Holy Spirit, which drew forth people of prayer in Wales who were in unconscious accord with the worldwide circles of prayer. The Spirit of God was manifestly brooding over the land, and doubtless there were many names of others that were recorded in heaven and who were burdened with a similar consciousness of need and who were drawn out in Spirit-taught prayer, both in the ordinary prayer meetings of the churches, in the young people's societies, and in their own personal alone time with God.

The Prophet of the Revival: Dean Howell

In Wales in the momentous year of 1902—the prayer movement year, we may call it—we see a figure standing out like Moses on Mount Pisgah, one who has since been called the "prophet of the revival," who beholds the land of far distances. He is the late Dean Howell of Saint David's, or "Llawdden," to use his bardic name. He was a dignitary of the Church of England, and, like Solomon, he had *"largeness of heart, even as the sand that is on the sea shore"* (1 Kings 4:29). He was regarded by all peoples as a saintly man of God, a patriot, preacher/orator, and a bard.

At the age of seventy-three, in the closing month of 1902, "Llawdden" looked out upon his beloved land in his faraway home on the farthest western point of the principality. Conscious of his standing on the brink of eternity, with earthborn things fading from his gaze and the light of heaven shining upon him, he sent out a message to his countrymen, since he was realized to be wondrously prophetic of the revival.

Howell first gave a vivid sketch of the spiritual dearth in the land, and then, in powerful language, he emphasized the only remedy—a spiritual awakening. He appealed to all to "create a circle of implorers" who would cry out to God in the words of Isaiah: *"Oh that thou wouldest rend the heavens, that thou wouldst come down"* (Isaiah 64:1). Then, beseeching his readers to consecrate themselves to make a revival the chief end of their desire, he closed with the following memorable words:

> Take notice, if it were known that this was my fast message to my fellow-countrymen throughout the length and breadth of Wales before being summoned to judgment, and the light of eternity already breaking over me, and it is this—the chief need of my country, and my dear nation at present is a spiritual revival through a special outpouring of the Holy Ghost.

The Dean's Last Message to Wales

The message was issued in a Welsh Magazine in January 1903 and caused a deep impression throughout the principality. It was his last message, for shortly after its issue, the aged Dean passed on to his heavenly reward.

"A spiritual revival through the outpouring of the Holy Ghost" was just what God had been leading His people to pray for all over the world, even in the principality of Wales. But before we watch the rising of the tide, we must again return to the prayer circle of Keswick in 1902.

In Keswick were found two Welsh ministers who had told how thirteen Welsh people gathered one afternoon in 1896 at the Keswick Convention for a prayer meeting for Wales, asking God Himself to give to Wales a similar convention for the deepening of the spiritual life. For six years, this petition lay before the Lord, until the seventh year—which in the Scriptures always speaks of God's fullness of time—when the Lord's time had come to answer.

Again, without using any of the usual "machinery," the Spirit of God immediately began to arrange a conference for Wales, by a series of steps of such remarkable guidance and wonderful coincidences, that insofar as anything can be said to be wrought of God, with the least touch of human hand, so it can be said that God Himself arranged and brought to fruition the convention, which became one of the channels for the rivers of life to enter Wales. When the aged Dean was asked whether, in his judgment, the time was ripe for such a conference for Wales in September of 1903, he stood, and with his hands raised and his eyes lifted heavenward, he said, "I am an old man on the edge of eternity, and I say that if such a conference could take place, God-given and not man-made, it would be an incalculable blessing to Wales."

From this time on, with much prayer and wise counsel, he entered into all the detailed arrangements for the conference. He gave his very last measures of strength and labors to the furthering of what he believed would bring about the "spiritual high tide" that he, at that very time, urged upon his countrymen as the "chief need" of Wales.

Meanwhile, the Spirit of God was working in the principality. The three ministers who banded together for prayer in May 1903 were conscious that the first step to receiving blessing for their churches was to get right with God themselves. They agreed to pray daily, but they could not see clearly the way to the better life. In their perplexity, they decided to write to a well-known London minister, begging him, if possible, to find the time to meet with a company of ministers in Glamorganshire to give them spiritual counsel and help. He replied that he could not come just then but told them of an upcoming conference, when he would gladly give them a private interview.

The First Llandrindod Convention in August 1903

At the very same time—in the spring of 1903 in a district in Glamorganshire—four young men, only eighteen years of age, were found on a mountainside holding a prayer meeting and pleading with

God for a revival in their church, which was in a cold and formal state where converts were few and far between. It transpired that these young men had held their prayer meetings on the mountain every night for a month! When this prayer circle became known, the majority of the church viewed the proceedings with suspicion, and some ignored or mocked the enthusiasm of the lads. But they continued to pray on the mountainside for two whole months; and, to the astonishment of the church, people who had never before visited any place of worship joined them and prayed with them! Some twelve or fourteen were now praying fervently for a revival, until at length the church members were touched, and all were moved with a Spirit of prayer and passion for souls. The meetings, composed of only four people at first, now increased to scores of people, and all of them testified to the power of God in a special manner.

This movement among the young people caused the pastor himself to search his own heart and life, asking himself whether he was fully surrendered to Christ and had received the Holy Spirit. Finally, he entered a new plane of spiritual experience and knowledge of the power of God.

There are many other indications of the river of God beginning to rise in the early months of 1903 and unmistakable signs of God working in preparation for some mighty movement of the Spirit. And at this crucial point, by the providence of God, came the long-prayed-for conference, which was held at Llandrindod Wells in August 1903.

The gatherings were strikingly representative; numbers of clergymen and ministers from all parts of the principality were present, together with some forty of the ministers and evangelists of the Forward Movement of the Presbyterian Church of Wales.[4] So noticeable was the ministerial attendance that a well-known missioner involuntarily remarked, "Wales may be the cradle of the evangelists for the coming revival!"

---

4. In many ways, the Forward Movement helped prepare the ground for the revival. At the time of this writing, it had been doing aggressive work in various centers in Wales for thirteen years, leading large numbers of converts into the full assurance of salvation and teaching them their need of the power of the Holy Spirit for service and soul-winning.

There was no set program for the meetings. The messages of the Lord's spokesmen bore directly upon the experimental aspect of the Holy Spirit's work in the believer. The putting away of all known sin, deliverance through identification with Christ in His death, and the definite reception of the Holy Spirit as an absolute necessity for all in the service of God were truths all emphasized and carried home to hearts by the power of God with such intensity that on the last two days, it was clear to all that the Spirit of God had come down into their midst.

And what of the group of three who had sought the help of the London minister? One wrote:

> Six of us went! But the history of that week can never be written—some believed, some doubted, some rebelled! But in a few days each one entered the promised land. We have met once a month ever since, coming from long distances, and we spend a quiet day with God. Our meetings have been indescribable, and we have had a number of Pentecosts.

Many of the ministers and workers returned to their various spheres of labors with new visions and new hopes. One said that a "new world" had opened to them—and they could not but lead others in! Local conventions were held in various places, and the ministers themselves became channels of blessing to their fellow ministers. One pastor wrote that he had come in contact with one of these ministers and saw at once that the minister had a spiritual experience that he himself had not, but which he had for months been seeking. It was not long before he, too, received the fullness of the Holy Spirit.

THREE

THE RIVER RISES IN AUTUMN

"Waters issued out from under the threshold."
—Ezekiel 47:1

On the day of Pentecost in Jerusalem, the Spirit of God came upon all members of the company gathered in the upper room; but when the multitude came together, it was Peter whom God chose to interpret what had happened to the people. But Peter could not have reaped the three thousand souls without the coservice of the one hundred and nineteen people who, along with him, had been filled with the Holy Spirit.

It has been said of the awakening in Wales that it is the "Acts of the Apostles up-to-date." And we cannot but think that this is so, not only in its manifestations, but in the way that the Pentecost has come upon the land. The movement is divine and heaven-born—and so was Pentecost. Yet in Jerusalem, the Spirit of God did not come first upon the multitudes, but *upon* the company in the upper room, and through them into the world in exact fulfillment of the Lord's words, *"I will send him unto you. And he, when he is come, will convict the world in respect of sin"* (John 16:7–8).

The law of the Holy Spirit's working has not changed, and we should doubtless find, if we were able to see all that is known to God, that He has had His "120" in Wales, who were prepared by Him to be channels for the outflowing of the Spirit in this great awakening. It is important for the children of God in other countries to realize this, so that they may yield themselves to Him and so that through them, He may send rivers of life to all nations in this day of His power.

The Life-Streams at New Quay

Let us look again from the Mount of God to watch the way that the life-streams began to break out in various places. We will turn our eyes first to New Quay, a little township in Cardiganshire, lying on the fringe of Cardigan Bay and fifteen miles from a railway station. Here in this out-of-the-way place, the Lord had been quietly preparing instruments for the coming Pentecost.

With a strange coincidence, which makes partnership with the Holy Spirit more romantic than any other earthly romance, the all-seeing Lord ordained that one of the mightiest rivers had its rise in the native land of a minister who once asked God to bless his land.

In the momentous year of 1902, a minister in New Quay—whose great-grandfather was one of the first band of preachers organized by Howell Harris—had been aroused to spiritual need by the words of a friend from India and of another who had told him that he feared he was "backsliding" (due to the absence of pathos in his voice when preaching!). Aroused to his need of greater blessing in his ministry, he sought the Lord through Bible studies and books on prayer, until at last he entered into a fuller life after reading Dr. Andrew Murray's book *With Christ in the School of Prayer.* The conviction grew upon him that the Spirit of God alone must save the church and the world.

He met another minister in November 1903, and they exchanged confidences over the burden on their hearts about the churches and their need of a more abundant life. Neither of these brothers had attended the Llandrindod Conference, but after prayer, they determined to present a request to the presbytery to hold a convention for the deepening of the spiritual life of the churches' members. The missioners chosen were three people who received, in the words of one, "fresh inspiration at Llandrindod." To these messengers, God again showed Himself far above the ways of men. The whole district of

South Cardiganshire is essentially Welsh, and there is no more than one English chapel within a twenty- to thirty-mile radius of another. Yet one of the messengers was a minister who rarely preached in anything but English; the other never preached in Welsh; and the third was a woman who had never spoken in public, except for once at the Forward Movement meetings following the conference at Llandrindod!

The convention was for delegates, and there was only one public meeting. But at this meeting, through the words of the handmaid of the Lord, the heart of a young girl was touched and its consequences could not have been dreamed of at the time.

Meanwhile, God had moved the pastor of the church that same November to begin a young people's meeting to counteract the worldly spirit growing among them.

One Sunday evening in January 1904, the pastor preached from the Scripture 1 John 5:4: *"This is the victory that hath overcometh the world, even our faith."* He was strangely drawn out to describe the world as he saw it before his spiritual vision. The young girl that had been touched a month before listened to his sermon, and that evening, she wended her way to his private house. Shy and retiring, she knew not how to tell him the burden on her soul. She walked around outside the house for half an hour, and then, gaining the courage to approach him, she entered the house and said, "Oh, how can I tell you! I cannot live like this. I saw the 'world' in your sermon tonight. I am under its feet. Help me." After some conversing, the pastor found that she thought she was saved, but she was afraid to yield entirely to the Savior and to declare Him as her Lord. "He may ask me difficult things," she said; and she would not commit herself to the lordship of Jesus Christ that night.

On the following Sunday morning, in February 1904, the Spirit of God bade the pastor to introduce some new feature in the young people's meeting held after the morning service. He asked them to share their personal testimonies, *definite* testimonies, as to what the Lord had done for their own souls.

One or two rose to speak, but they did not share their testimony. It was just then that the same young girl—shy, nervous, and intelligent—stood up in tears, and with clasped hands, she said with deep pathos, "Oh, I love Jesus Christ with all my heart." Instantly, the Spirit of God appeared to have fallen upon the gathering, and all were deluged with tears. It was the beginning of a visible manifestation of the Spirit. It broke out in life-streams and eventually touched thousands of souls.

As it was at Pentecost, the blessing was soon noised abroad. Doors began to open on every hand, and the young people, led by their minister, conducted meetings throughout the southern half of the county, the Lord manifesting His power in them. But at that time, the world knew little of what was going on.

The Second Convention at Llandrindod in August 1904

In August 1904, the second convention at Llandrindod took place, and the testimony meeting revealed how deep a work had been wrought in 1903. A minister wrote to *Y Goleuad*—a Welsh paper—saying that at the 1904 conference, "many saw a door of hope for revival in Wales in the near future." Referring to the testimony meeting, he said,

> It was a luxury to hear ministers and laymen giving expression to the change that had taken place in their ministry and in their own personal lives since the convention of 1903. Reference was made to a more intense consecration, to habits set aside, to a fuller dependence on the power of the Holy Spirit, and the many souls born in consequence thereof. Some testified that the Bible was a new book to them; others that prayer was easier and more powerful than it used to be…It is manifest that better days are about to dawn, and blessed are those believers who are willing now to consecrate themselves as worthy mediums for the Holy Ghost in the next revival.

In that momentous week in 1904, the Spirit of God broke forth again in glorious power. None will ever forget the closing morning meeting, when, overcome by the revelation of the fullness of redemption purchased for the sinner by Jesus Christ and with hands raised and bowed heads, the audience sang again and again and again, "Crown Him Lord of All." Neither will the message that night on "exuberance of life in Jesus Christ" ever be forgotten. Truly, God was leading His people into an open vision of Himself and preparing them for the exuberant life, which He has since shown in object lesson before the eyes of the world.

All through 1903 and 1904, the underground currents were quietly deepening and sometimes breaking out to the surface, until the time drew near when the floodgates opened and the Spirit of God broke out upon the land like a tidal wave, sweeping up all things before it; or, to use another illustration, like a forest fire, consuming all things it touched.

The New Church Arises

We have seen the beginning of the life-streams in New Quay in February 1904. Let us now look at some of the ministers who entered into the Spirit-filled life in August 1903. They tell of a midnight prayer meeting at the 1904 conference, when they all consecrated themselves afresh to God for His use and asked the Lord to raise up someone to usher in the revival! A month later, two of their churches were in the midst of a mighty awakening, when scores of people were converted!

One minister returned to his people and urged upon every believer the fullness of the Spirit. This soon aroused attention, and the subject was talked about by the colliers at work. Some opposed, but some yielded, and several young men surrendered to the Holy Spirit.

At the end of September, prayer meetings were held on every weeknight, until the schoolroom was filled, and they had to adjourn to the chapel, where again they gathered every night for three weeks longer. The prayer meetings were then intermingled with testimony meetings, and afterward, special services were conducted by one of the ministers who had entered the Spirit-filled life. At these services, fifty attendees accepted the Savior, and large numbers of young people received in actual experience their Pentecost. By the end of the year, one hundred twenty souls were added to the Lord.

Another minister who entered the Spirit-filled life in 1903 returned to his church, fervently praying for an outpouring of the Spirit. Slowly, signs pointed toward better things approaching. People in the church who had taken offense at the words or actions of others were reconciled. Unity prepared the way of the Lord.

On November 20, 1904, the Spirit of God broke out. The pastor had been preaching at a mission station in the morning, but after passing the mother-church on his way home, he entered and found that the service was still in progress. But something had occurred! There was not a dry eye in the place! The people were shedding tears and smiling at the same time. One of the elders, in a broken voice, said that they had experienced a most wonderful meeting. The Holy Spirit had come in such mighty power that they decided to dispense with Sunday school and sermons, and spend the day in prayer and praise.

"Under normal conditions it would be necessary to give due notice of re-arrangements of this kind, and to have them sanctioned by a church meeting," wrote the pastor, "but now the Holy Spirit took possession heeding not our arrangements, and no one had the courage or the desire to protest!" From this time on, meetings were held every night, and some of the young people became possessed by the Spirit to such a remarkable degree that the "acts of the apostles became more intelligible" to all. Many fully surrendered themselves to Christ the King and shared soul-stirring testimonies. Those who, up to this time, had taken but a passive interest in the work of the church sprang forward and became bold witnesses for Christ. Outside meetings were organized, where even young women raised their voices in testimony, and those who had been too diffident to take part in public service now did not hesitate to speak even to drunkards coming out of bars and to kneel down and pray for them in the open streets.

Another minister returned to his church bearing witness to the Spirit-filled life, and signs of blessing appeared in September 1903, as a deep thirst for better things slowly grew among the members. In July 1904, the pastor commenced a special meeting after the ordinary evening service, particularly for those who desired to live the Spirit-filled life. The Holy Spirit came upon that meeting in such manifest power that all present were overwhelmed, and remarkable testimonies were given afterward by many. On a later Sunday evening, the Spirit of God broke forth again in the ordinary service.

Strong men were broken down and said afterward that they felt as if they must shout to relieve their pent-up feelings. Several young men gave themselves to Christ in this service. Sunday after Sunday, the place was filled by the Holy Spirit, and several conversions took place. At the close of one service held in October, all who desired to consecrate themselves to the Lord and to go out and seek the lost were asked to meet in the schoolroom; and here the revival began. Souls were saved night after night for the succeeding weeks.

"But," wrote the pastor,

although we had completed ten weeks of prayer meetings, and many souls were gathered in, I still felt the church as a whole had not received her Pentecost. Early in December 1904, in a memorable prayer meeting, several crossed the line and entered the promised land. Some men were so literally filled with the Spirit that others could have said "They are drunk with new wine." A great passion for souls took possession of many hearts from this time, and in one week seventy souls were gathered in. Many made public confession of sins, and consecrated themselves to Christ. After 11 o'clock one Saturday night, ten men yielded to the Savior, and over one hundred and fifty confessed Christ ere 1904 closed. The whole movement, without doubt, had its origin in my own awakening. After I surrendered all conscious sin and yielded entirely to Christ, a new power was immediately felt in my ministry. Now I have a *new* church, with a large number of men and women who have been filled with the Holy Spirit, and are used to winning souls.

FOUR

THE TIDAL WAVE SWEEPS
THE COUNTRY

"The waters were risen, waters to swim in."
—Ezekiel 47:5

We now go back to Cardiganshire to read the outcome of a blessing given at New Quay in February 1904. In September 1904, the Reverend Seth Joshua, the connection evangelist of the Forward Movement, visited New Quay for a mission and found the Holy Spirit working in such a remarkable way that he at once felt it betokened a great revival. The presence of the Spirit in the meetings was like a wind moving upon the people. (See John 3:8.) The singing, prayers, testimonies, and exhortations were all full of vital breath. The meetings were closed two or three times, and some people cried for mercy or broke out in joyful thanksgiving. Strong men and women wept under the power of one young girl's prayer. Many of the young people had manifestly received a baptism of power. The love among the believers was intense, and the tenderness of prayer for one another irresistible.

From New Quay, the evangelist went to Newcastle Emlyn, wherein there was a preparatory school for students entering the ministry. At the services conducted by Mr. Joshua, some students manifestly received the power of the Holy Spirit, among whom was Sydney Evans, the fellow student and friend of the one whom God had been preparing as a special instrument for the Pentecost, now close at hand.

The Young Evan Roberts

In the same preparatory school was Evan Roberts, a young collier student of twenty-six years of age who was preparing to enter the ministry. For eleven years, he had prayed for a revival; and for thirteen years, he had prayed for the fullness of the Spirit.

A simple phrase dropped by a deacon in a church meeting thirteen years before had given him a yearning to know the Holy Spirit. "Be faithful," said the deacon. "What if the Spirit descended, and you were absent!" So, through all weathers and difficulties, refusing to be tempted by the boys and the boats on the river near his home, the lad wended his way to prayer meetings and other chapel services, year after year.

Evan Roberts came from a typical Welsh home and was the son of godly parents. At twelve years of age, he became his father's right-hand man in the coal mine, and shortly after, he commenced regular work underground in the colliery. He was never without his Bible, which he studied on his breaks at work. And so the time went by this way until one night in the spring of 1904, when God seemed to have drawn near to him in a very special way. He said that as he prayed by his bedside that night, he was taken up into a great expanse—without space or time—into communion with God.

This was manifestly a crisis in his spiritual life, for hitherto, he says, God was to him "a faraway God," and he was afraid of Him. But after this, the Lord awakened him night after night, a little after one o'clock, and took him up into divine fellowship with Him for about four hours. He would sleep until nine o'clock, when again he was taken up into communion with God until about noon in the day. These intervals of sacred fellowship with the Lord lasted three months, and then came the time for him to go to the preparatory school at Newcastle Emlyn in September 1904.

The Spirit Baptism of Evan Roberts

At this time, a convention was being held at Blaenannerch, some eight miles from Newcastle Emlyn, and the messengers who were sharing the Lord's message were the same three who had been sent to New Quay at the close of 1903.

The Reverend Seth Joshua had now commenced his mission, and on a Thursday morning, he took a party of about twenty young people—including a group from New Quay, as well as Evan Roberts and Sydney Evans—to Blaenannerch to attend the meetings. The Lord worked in that horse-drawn vehicle on that early morning drive as they sung, "It is coming—It is coming—The power of the Holy Ghost—I receive it—I receive it—The power of the Holy Ghost." Singing and praising, they reached Blaenannerch in time for the seven o'clock service, which was being conducted by one of the missioners.

Evan Roberts was already deeply moved, but he broke down when at the close Mr. Joshua led in prayer and used the words, "Plyg ni, O Arglwydd"—"Bend us, O Lord." The soul in travail heard no words but these. *This is what you need*, whispered the Spirit of God to Evan. "Bend me, O Lord," he cried, but even then, the fire had not yet fallen.

At the nine o'clock meeting, the Spirit of God led one and then another to pray, and then Mr. Roberts said, "I fell on my knees with my arms over the seat in front of me, and the tears freely flowed. I cried, 'Bend me! Bend me! Bend us!' What bent me was God commending His love, and I not seeing anything in it to commend." The Holy Spirit had come and melted his whole being by a revelation of the love of God at Calvary, for "*God commendeth his own love toward us, in that, while we were yet sinners, Christ died for us*" (Romans 8:5).

The Tidal Wave

The young man returned to Newcastle Emlyn and prayed to God to give him the seal of six others set on fire for God, and the six were given. Then the Holy Spirit bade him return to his own people and speak to them, but he did not obey, although he continued to grow more and more troubled and ill at ease. One Sunday in chapel, he could not fix his mind on the service, for always before him—as in a vision—he saw the schoolroom in his own village, and all the young people and his old companions sitting in rows while he addressed them. He told of how he shook his head impatiently and sought to drive all these thoughts away, but God would give him no rest. They came back again and again, and the Holy Spirit's whisper became clearer and clearer: *Go and speak to these people.*

At last, the pressure grew so strong that he could no longer resist, and he said he would go. Instantly, the glory of the Lord so filled the chapel that he *"could not see for the glory of that light"* (Acts 22:11). After this, the young man went to an aged minister to ask him whether this was of God or of the devil. He replied that the devil was not given to sending people to work like this—he must obey the heavenly vision.

So in obedience to the voice of God, the young student went to Loughor. What God worked in him we will see later on. We will first pause a moment to see how God answers prayer—this young student's prayer in particular. In the horse-drawn carriage that morning on the way to Blaenannerch, Mr. Joshua told of how it had been laid upon him four years before to ask the Lord to take a lad from the coal mine or from the field, even as He took Elisha, to revive His work in Wales. He prayed that God would raise an instrument through whom human pride would be humbled—not one from Cambridge, lest it would minister to their pride, nor one from Oxford University, lest it would feed the intellectualism of the church. Not once had this prayer been mentioned to anyone until that morning, and it was then revealed, without anyone knowing that the very instrument God had chosen was listening to his words.

Let us recall, too, the midnight prayer meeting at Llandrindod just two months before, when the Lord was asked to raise some special instrument to usher in the revival. Yes, God answers prayer.

So Evan Roberts went to Loughor, his native land, early in November 1904. And He says that he consulted the pastor of his church, who told him that he would try to see what he could do, but warned him that he would find the ground stony and the task hard!

And so the young people in his town came together, and they all sat before him as he had been shown in his vision by God. At first, they did not seem to be touched, but soon, the Spirit of God began to work, and six came out for Christ. Then the Pentecost began. Soul after soul came forward, and the most extraordinary results followed. The whole community was shaken. The meetings lasted until four in the morning, and at six o'clock, the people were awakened by the sounds of the crowds going to the early morning prayer meeting. The work went on until, as a local minister said, the entire population had been transformed into a praying multitude—men and women of whom he had despaired had voluntarily come to Christ. The lives of hundreds of colliers and tinsmiths were transformed. The men went straight to the chapel from the mills, and the bars were practically deserted.

On November 10, the first public reference to these remarkable scenes was made in a secular Welsh paper, which, from that time on, and to the wonderment of all, devoted columns to the reporting of the work, and did much in the providence of God to noise abroad what God had been doing among His people. Other secular papers did the same, and all men marveled at the sovereign power of God in thus moving the secular press to report the work of God!

From Loughor, "the Revivalist," as the young student had begun to be called, went on to Trecynon and other villages, manifestly carrying on the crest of a mighty wave of the Spirit, which swept like a cleansing tide through the mining valleys of Glamorganshire. Everywhere, the people thronged in multitudes to hear this Spirit-filled young student!

It is said that he spoke at Loughor with impassioned oratory, but once the overflowing stream had broken out, the Spirit of God appeared to put aside preaching in exchange for the voice of testimony. The burden of the message of the Spirit-filled souls in the days of Pentecost is summed up in two verses: 1) *"The God of our fathers raised up Jesus, whom ye slew, hanging him on a tree. Him did God exalt"* (Acts 5:30–31) and 2) *"We are witnesses of these things"* (Acts 5:32). And this was the Holy Spirit's message now through His people, as

He bore cowitness by working signs and wonders among the thronging multitudes.

Under the constraint of an unseen power, the chapels were filled with eager people at all hours of the day, and the services took their own course under the control of the Holy Spirit, presiding as, in Andrew Murray's words, "the executive power of the Godhead." Prayers, testimonies, and singing broke out in seeming disorder, but yet it was acknowledged by all to be in the most harmonious order. The revivalist would enter during the meeting, sometimes unknown to those present, until he rose with some word for the people. The burden of his message would be along the lines of "obey the Holy Spirit." And when someone in the meeting would break out into prayer while he was speaking, he would calmly "give place," and show to others that he acknowledged the presidency of the One who was greater than he.

Perhaps Mr. Roberts would "test" the meeting at some point, putting it up beside the four definite steps salvation that the Holy Spirit had given to him to urge upon the people:

1. The past must be cleared by confessing sin to God; and every wrong of man put right.

2. Every doubtful thing in the life must be put away.

3. Prompt and implicit obedience to the Holy Spirit.

4. Public confession of Christ.

The forgiveness of others was often emphasized as an essential to receiving forgiveness, as well as the distinction between the Holy Spirit's work in conversion and in baptizing the believer.

In truth, the revivalist was sharing the full gospel as it was preached at Pentecost; and like Peter's message, it received the cowitness of the Holy Spirit and produced Pentecostal results. "Repent" means to change your mind toward God and to put away all wrongs toward your neighbor. As you repent, the remission of sins will then be given you, and you will receive the Holy Spirit if you obey Him and publicly bear witness to Christ. This is the message that he taught to his listeners.

Indescribable scenes took place at these meetings. Sometimes, a torrent of prayer and then of song would sweep over the audience, and hundreds of souls would rise to declare their surrender to God; the congregation bursting out into joyous thanksgiving in hymns of gladness.

But the revivalist's special burden was always for the church. "Bend the church, and save the world," was his cry. The word *bend* in Welsh conveys the meaning of submission to God and the taking away of all resistance to His will. And the revivalist's one aim seemed to be to get the Christians right with God, so that the Spirit might break out in converting power upon the unsaved. And Calvary was the power for both the sinner and the saved. The revivalist would break down in heart-anguished sobbing when he thought or spoke of the theme. "You would not be cold if you had come here from Calvary," he would say. In many of his prayers, he'd say, "Thanks, thanks for Calvary." The hymns rang with Calvary.

One of the hymns most often sung was "Pen Calfaria"—"The Mount of Calvary"—an exultant song of triumph telling of Christ's victory over death and hell at the cross. Another hymn that was sung with melting power was "Dyma Gariad"—"Here Is Love." The people sang without books, for these hymns had been in their memories from childhood; but now they were quickened and used by the Spirit, ringing out as never before.

Many of the "sweet singers of Wales" were drawn by the Spirit of God into His service and those who were bowed in prayer would often hear these singers with sweet warbling voices like a nightingale's trill breaking out into a hymn. A revival it truly became. Souls were sung to Christ and exulted over in song when won. The Spirit of gladness and praise filled all hearts, as thousands rejoiced in a newfound assurance of salvation. People who were rarely touched by ordinary means came to Christ, and quickly the world heard of the results.

Magistrates were presented with white gloves in several places because there were no cases. Bars were forsaken. Rowdiness was changed to soberness. Oaths ceased to be heard—so that, it was said, the horses could no longer understand the language of their drivers in the coal mines. The reading of light literature was exchanged for Bible reading, and shops were cleared of their stocks of Bibles and Testaments. Prayer meetings were held in collieries underground, as well as in trains and trams and all kinds of places.

The whole world bore testimony to these practical evidences of the power of God. When Peter healed the lame man, the onlookers could not help but believe: *"And seeing the man which was healed standing with them, they could say nothing against it"* (Acts 4:14). Many who were previously skeptical of the practical power of the Christian faith said, *"A notable miracle hath been wrought…and we cannot deny it"* (Acts 4:16). And so it was with the revival. For instance, managers of factories bore witness that the amount of work turned out by the men since the revival had been more than they had known in previous years, and magistrates did not hesitate to make known their approval of the ethical fruits of the awakening.

Far and wide the influences spread, affecting all classes. Miners' associations decided to no longer hold their conferences on licensed premises. Political meetings had to be postponed, and members of Parliament were found taking part in revival meetings. Football teams were disbanded because the men had been converted. The Spirit of God did His own work of convicting, and many people were the evidence of His power working through hymn and testimony. A young man would return his prize medal and diploma because he had gained it unfairly. A grocer would return money that he had picked up in his shop and kept, although knowing the one who dropped it. Long-standing debts were paid. Stolen goods were returned. Prizefighters, gamblers, and publicans had other attractions now. A theatrical company felt it necessary to depart from one district, as there was no hope of bringing in audiences, for all the "world" was praying. In one accord, the converts put aside "the drink," and the temperance workers saw the Spirit of God accomplish in three months what they had labored to do for forty years! At the conclusion of a service, dozens of young men would be seen marching to the front to sign the pledge.

The mighty tidal wave swept to and fro—men knew not how or why. The Spirit of God found His own channels, and districts unvisited by Mr. Evan Roberts had extraordinary manifestations of the power of God. Lists of converts were sent to the newspapers, giving a record of professed conversions of over 70,000 names by December 1904—only two months after the life-streams broke out in Loughor; the number reached over 85,000 by the end of March 1905! Many of the young people were thrust out by the Lord to share in the service: Mr. Sydney Evans; Mr. Dan Roberts, and many others led revival meetings with the manifest blessing of God. Visitors from all parts of Britain and the Continent began to flock to Wales to see the "great sight" of God breaking forth in supernatural power upon the sons of men.

FIVE

THE LIFE-STREAMS IN SOUTHERN WALES

"Every thing shall live whithersoever the river cometh."
—Ezekiel 47:9

The Overflowing Streams Through Various Channels

The glimpses we have had into the preparatory work of the Spirit explain why the river of God broke out in so many districts at the same time in November 1904. Taking a bird's-eye view of South Wales, we might look at each of these instances and watch the rising tide.

Carmarthen

In Carmarthen, we find the Spirit of God at work in preparation for months beforehand, some of the ministers of the town having entered the Spirit-filled life in 1903; afterward, one became a missioner at the New Quay Convention, and in the months that followed, many others became missioners at both the New Quay Convention and the Blaenannerch Convention.

The first preparation of the Holy Spirit was drawing together the Free Churches in unity, until early in November, when He began to manifest His presence in a supernatural display of His power. The churches had unitedly convened a convention for the deepening of the spiritual life in the members; but on the Sabbath evening preceding the convention, the Spirit of God broke out in three places of worship in the town, strong men weeping and young and old men praying and praising in a most unheard of fashion.

In one church on Monday night, about eighty adults were studying Luke chapter 4 in a Bible class, when, suddenly, there grew upon the whole company a vision of Christ unique in His person and claims. All began to pray and praise God, unaware to themselves, crying with joy and praying, as one said, "It was as if our souls would escape from our bodies."

A Convention was held the same week, and another the week after, in Welsh only, for the benefit of the country churches. Delegates came in large numbers, and the floodgates of heaven were opened in these churches. Between the meetings that second week, it was said that in every classroom and available corner of the chapel grounds, groups of women, young people, ministers, or elderly men were seen in prayer, many sobbing and pleading with God in utter oblivion of all that was around. On one night, the whole congregation marched in procession to the market square for a jubilant outside service of praise.

Morriston

In Morriston, we hear of the minister of one church, consisting of over five hundred members, who was deeply burdened over his people—so burdened that he had sent in his resignation and determined to seek a secular calling. There had been trouble among the deacons, and a meeting was called to deal with the offending officers. But at this stage, the pastor came across John MacNeil's book *The Spirit-Filled Life*. It was a message from God to him, and it revealed to him his need.

Just then, he heard of the revival flame bursting out at Mountain Ash, and he went across to attend one of the meetings. At the close of the service, alone in a back street, he surrendered fully to God; and on the following Sunday, he told his people what had happened to him. The Spirit of God at once broke out. The pastor's resignation was not accepted. The deacons had no need to be dealt with. The overflowing stream reached many souls, until, on the last Sunday of 1904, one hundred thirty-eight were received into church fellowship, with one hundred eighty-five converts registered in five weeks.

District Close to Loughor

In another district, not far from Loughor, the vicar of the parish tells of an indefinable influence at work for some time before November, which very quickly reached full tide when the Spirit of God broke forth in the land. He wrote that in the opening services of the parish church on November 4, there was not a single dry eye among the congregation, and at that time, they had not even held any revival services yet.

Two laymen in this church seem to be men filled with the Spirit, having great power in prayer and utterance. And before long, about seventy parishioners had been led to the Savior. After-meetings were held, when quiet boys and girls, twelve years old and older, prayed or sang, and a marvelous change was seen in the lives of the people.

Swansea

In the Swansea district, we hear of church after church, from both the Church of England and Nonconformist groups, where the Spirit of God broke out in rivers of life. In some cases, this happened unexpectedly, and in others, it happened after a long and faithful preaching of the gospel or Calvary or the fullness of the Spirit for every believer as promised by the Lord.

Neath

In the Neath district, we find the Holy Spirit moving in a large mission hall holding two thousand people. The pastor received the "anointing" some thirteen years ago, and hence was ready for the tide when it came. Hearing of the blessing at Loughor early in November, a prayer meeting was held every other week, and the members asked God to send a Pentecost upon the work. During one of the nights of prayer, the Spirit of God dealt with the church members, and then, at a Sunday evening service, the blessing broke out.

At the close of the pastor's address, before he could even ask for decisions, men and women rose from the crowded congregation amid intense stillness and no excitement, and pressed into the inquiry rooms until they were filled. One hundred nineteen souls had found the Lord. Thirty-eight souls were given the next night, and the reaping went on until over a thousand converts were gathered in, among whom were many men and women had never gone to a place of worship; many who had been to prison; drunkards, prizefighters, gamblers, and one clog dancer who had won gold medals in his calling. There were women who were quite drunk that would stagger into the meetings and be soundly converted while standing in the hall.

How truly the work was of God was seen in many cases. One publican offered a convert a fortnight's free drink if he would break away, but he answered, "No, I have had enough of it, for it kept me in Swansea jail." Another man passing a bar saw the landlady come out and hold up a pint of beer, saying, "Come along," but the convert held up his Bible and replied, "No, we're going with this now. This is the key to heaven, and that to hell!" Other churches in this town have also much to tell of the Lord's grace and blessing.

Bridgend

In the Bridgend district, we find again the Spirit of God at work many months before the spiritual high tide came upon the land. Several of the ministers received the power of the Holy Spirit in August 1903. One was the pastor of a prominent church, which had the worldly reputation that was an almost insuperable obstacle to aggressive Christian work. But when he entered the Spirit-filled life, his church immediately felt the change. Some members were attracted, while many declared the standard of life he called for to be too high.

At last, in 1904, there commenced remarkable "*demonstration*[s] *of the Spirit*" (1 Corinthians 2:4), and the Spirit of God faced the pastor with the painful duty of dealing personally with the officers of the church. Among the deacons was an able solicitor, a man well-known in his profession and prominent in the political world, whose whole life (afterward acknowledged by himself) was an utterly worldly one. A private interview was arranged, when the Lord stood with the faithful pastor and spoke through him in such power that the deacon was broken down and came as a penitent to the foot of the cross.

Not many days after, he called together his fellow deacons and told them he had found Christ and was a new man. The same testimony was given to the Bible class and afterward to the public congregation; and each time he spoke of the mercy of the Lord and the music that filled his heart, his hearers were deeply moved. His fellow deacons at once consecrated themselves to the Lord, and the effect upon the church was as the "breaking down of an obstructing dam up among the sources of power." A flood tide of the Spirit broke out among the congregation, and a fervent piety and passion for souls took the place of the former deadness in the people. Not only was the church blessed, but the conversion of souls—like that of Saul of Tarsus—produced great effect in the district. The pastor publicly confessed that the change meant to him that the whole outlook of his life was transformed, affecting his home and his business; and in the latter sphere, his numerous clients who owned pubs were requested to find another advocate for their interests.

It was not long after this that this church had its Pentecost. On a Sabbath morning, the pastor read the second chapter of Acts, and a woman rose and said, "Let me seal that with my testimony." Then she told how the Lord had come to her in the night and told her He had given her a mission to speak for Him. Her husband sat by her side sobbing, as the woman spoke with her face lit up for the first time in public. Testimonies followed until the whole church was moved. At night, the Spirit of God so worked among the people that in different parts of the building, many fell on their knees crying out, while rough men of the town rose from every side and accepted Christ.

This Pentecost Sunday was followed by a steady work of the Spirit among church members and the unsaved. Scores of inquirers poured in, week after week, drawn by the Spirit of God, many of them characters who were long ago pronounced hopeless. And it has been an affecting sight to see the solicitor and leading politician pleading with rough and fallen men and women, as a brother and a fellow sinner. God has been using him mightily in winning souls to Christ. No less than one hundred fifty converts have been gathered in to this church, giving every token of a deep inward change of heart.

In another district, the River of Life broke out sometime in the middle of November. A minister who knew the indwelling Spirit had visited in the past July to do some preparatory work. And when the Holy Spirit visited this church months later, many members then entered the Spirit-filled life and were prepared to understand the work of the Spirit when He came in Pentecostal power. One Saturday night, a marvelous prayer meeting preceded the opening of the floodgates of heaven, and it was not long before two hundred sixty converts were added to the church. Adding to the blessing among the unsaved, many of the Christians who had opposed the message of the Spirit-filled life in July now publicly confessed that they had been wrong, and some gave remarkable testimonies of the Holy Spirit's working in their lives.

Dowlais

In Dowlais, the River of Life had commenced to flow some time in the summer of 1904 upon the visit of some to New Quay. In one Dowlais church, the pastor writes that for months, the Holy Spirit had paid visits to the church that were "wondrously powerful and significant." At several distinct periods, and without any apparent reason, the congregation members would simultaneously burst into tears. The pastor himself had often sought with tears at the throne of grace a greater influx of power in his own life. At the close of August, three ministers who knew the Spirit-filled life conducted services in the church, and many received the filling of the Spirit after a definite surrender to Christ; and God at once began to use them powerfully.

The pastor writes that his own life became a radically changed one—his spiritual sphere was transfigured and made very real to him. The River of Life flowed on from that time in August, and conversions took place at every meeting, until, by the close of 1904, one hundred seventy had been added to the Lord, and more and more believers were brought into full surrender to Christ and into the knowledge of the indwelling Holy Spirit.

Monmouthshire

Passing on to Monmouthshire, the pastor of one church writes that after his return from the 1904 Llandrindod Conference, he did not lead one prayer meeting, church meeting, or any other service without urging the message concerning the wholehearted reception of the Spirit upon his people. And in October, two ministers who had experienced the Spirit-filled life came to conduct special services, and the whole church was transformed—the entire diaconate receiving blessing. Seventy-four converts were also gathered in, and in the afternoon meetings for Christians, three women who had come from another church entered into the fullness of blessing, receiving a baptism of love for souls. These became channels of the life-streams in their own church, where two hundred converts were quickly won to Christ.

In another district, we find special services of the same class, when everyone who attended the afternoon meetings surrendered fully to Christ and received the Holy Spirit, while souls were brought to Christ at every meeting. These services were held at the very time that the Spirit of God broke out in Loughor.

Cardiff

In Cardiff, God orchestrated one of the romantic coincidences so frequently experienced by souls led by the Spirit. In October 1904, a man who was called out from the prayer company in Chicago for the service of God in "worldwide revival" conducted a great mission in Cardiff. And there is evidence that he was used of God especially to touch ministers and workers in his messages concerning the Spirit-filled life. Thus was the Lord through many channels preparing His people.

When the high tide came upon the land, we find a most unique work of God in the center of Cardiff, in a large chapel filled night after night with people of all classes and some of the very hopeless outcasts of the town brought by the power of God into newness of life. Agnostics have given testimony to faith in Jesus Christ, and drunkards have been delivered from their bonds. Midnight meetings were held, revealing the horrors of sin and the power of Christ to save. Other churches in the town were also deeply moved by God, as in the town of Penarth, another center of blessing, where over six hundred converts were added to one church. Drunkards, thieves, gamblers, and others were rescued and are now among the best workers in the service of Christ.

The Spirit broke out in November when no special evangelist had visited the church, which had been praying for revival for about two years. The pastor tells of how God prepared him by having him read books on the Spirit-filled life, which life he entered upon at the aforesaid mission in Cardiff in October.

These instances—and they are but *instances* of the way that the Spirit of God worked in places far distant from each other—show that He was moving in different parts of Wales at the same time, and the life-streams which had been quietly rising appear to have silently joined the bigger current in November 1904, creating a high tide that swept over the land. We find that all sections of the church were affected by it, for the Holy Spirit is no respecter of denominations any more than persons, and He freely worked in every place where He was welcomed and was given room.

In watching the course of the mighty river of God, which swept from Loughor through the mining districts of South Wales, we have summarized briefly some of the effects upon the masses and upon the world. Let us now look out upon the whole of South Wales and view the broad effects of the Pentecost upon the people of God.

The General Effect on the Churches in Southern Wales

What has the spiritual high tide accomplished? It not only swept down the mining valleys as a torrent, cleansing and healing as it went, but it silently enveloped the machinery of the churches, and lifted them, so to speak, into a new spiritual sphere. The traditional bonds of years were broken. Prejudices of the past vanished. Not only in the meetings held by revivalists, but in ordinary services, the Spirit of God—hitherto often considered but an influence—was honored as the third Person of the Trinity and given His place of presidency over the church. Pastors allowed the services to take any form that might arise from the movement of the Spirit. Anyone might rise to speak or lead in prayer without fear, and sermons were put aside when the need arose.

In the overflowing tide, denominational barriers between the people of God were submerged, as when the sea sweeps in upon the shore and swallows up in its glorious fullness, all the pools of seawater separated far from one another on the sand. Wondrous scenes were witnessed that must have caused the heavenly spheres to ring with the joy of the angels. Churches that were on unbrotherly terms for many years were reconciled and united and organized meetings. In one case, the two ministers shook hands before the people.

In some districts—if only we could say all—clergy and their Free Church brethren freely met together to worship God. Families were reunited; long-severed friends reconciled; children were restored to parents; offended church members retook their places among the people of the Lord. And in place after place, the ministers' fraternal meetings became fraternal in very truth, for hearts flowed together in true fellowship in the presence of the Lord.

With the Spirit of unity and love came also the Spirit of sacrifice. Churches up to that point that were divided on the question of whether to use fermented wine at the table of the Lord unanimously decided to put away all of their perceivable danger of the weaker brethren. In other churches, large numbers of old members signed the pledge for the sake of the weaker ones rescued from the drink fiend, and in another church, we read of members vacating their own pews in the body of the building and retiring to the gallery, that the area might be used for the aggressive work of gathering in the souls.

We find also a wondrous Spirit of liberty, which strikingly bears the marks of Pentecost, for in the surcharged atmosphere of the upper room in Jerusalem, all began to speak. The tongues of the young people, hitherto shy before their elders, were loosed to speak or pray without fear of rebuke. It is now no uncommon thing to see a young girl of eighteen years speaking under the evident control of the Holy Spirit, while in the big pew sit ministers and elders oftentimes with tears coursing down their faces. And the servants and hand-maidens are prophesying, as foretold by Joel.

Again, we find that the prophesying takes the form of witnessing—the special mark of Pentecost. In Wales for many years, it had been considered too sacred a thing to speak of the inner dealings of God; yet suddenly, we see that all this had changed, and sermons were put aside for testimony and public confession of what the Lord had done for the soul.

Another remarkable change occurred in many people's attitude toward the prayer meeting. It was, up to that point, shunted for any social event, as one had said; and none but the elders, when called upon, solemnly took part in it! But new social events stood aside for the prayer meetings, which were more attractive than all else. The Spirit of prayer, too, was given in a much travail for souls, and narrow bounds were swept away, as prayer was made for all the nations.

We have referred elsewhere to the way that the Holy Spirit made Calvary the center and the source of blessing, and there are many traces of a remarkable revelation of the cross to the *"eyes of your heart"* (Ephesians 1:18). An evangelist told how he was praying with others in a certain house one day, when the Lord revealed Himself to a servant girl in a "clear vision of the cross with herself at the base"; and she shared that her "experience and power in the service which followed was most touching." In a meeting, too, at Carmarthen, a worker rose and asked why she saw the cross of Calvary before her vision night and day.

There are other Pentecostal marks discernible in places where the Spirit of God has worked in mighty power, in signs and wonders that are worked among the people. These signs and wonders include miracles of physical deliverance for souls wrecked by the demon of strong drink. One convert, who had been a gambler and drunkard, with his bodily frame shattered by his life, gave testimony that since the day of his conversion he had been perfectly restored to his normal health. Another who had not been sober one weekend for thirty-five years said he could not now smell alcoholic liquor without sickness—the revulsion was so great.

In this day of His power, we find others, too, proving the healing power of God. A minister told how he was taken ill in the midst of his work, but he appealed to the Lord and found himself instantly healed! He did not hesitate to bear witness to this in a meeting, when quickly many others sprang to their feet and said what the Lord had done for them in the same way, one being a minister's wife who entered the Spirit-filled life only a few months before. In another meeting, the power of the Spirit was so intense that the missioners could not *pray* for deliverance for the souls held in bondage by the evil one, but they were constrained irresistibly to *command* the adversary to release his captives, and numbers were thus set free by the power of God.

If we speak of the converts swept in by the spiritual high tide, we might describe them in the very words of Scripture! They are the ones who have *"received his word"* (Acts 2:41) and have *"continued stedfastly in…fellowship…and the prayers"* (verse 42)—the great numbers who were baptized and received to the table of the Lord. *"All that believed"* (Acts 2:44) now continue *"with one accord"* (verse 46) in the various church meetings and are filled *"with gladness and singleness of heart"* (verse 46), for they have lost their desire for the things of the world, which they have come out of, and now long to fully serve the Lord! They are *"praising God* [with *"psalms and hymns and spiritual songs"* (Ephesians 5:19)], *and having favour with all the people. And the Lord* [adds] *to them day by day* [others who are also] *saved"* (Acts 2:47).

But it must be remembered that these converts are but babes, many utterly untaught, although born into the kingdom of God in this day of Pentecostal power. (See 1 Corinthians 3:1.) It remains for the pastors to lead them on into the fullness of the life in the Spirit, so that they become established in the knowledge of God, and the Church of God in Wales is established in deed and truth after the pattern of Pentecost.

SIX

THE LIFE-STREAMS IN NORTHERN WALES

"Northward…behold, there ran out waters."
—Ezekiel 47:2

We have watched the rivers of living water breaking out in many directions in South Wales. Let us now turn our eyes to North Wales and see how the divine Spirit has been working in the northern part of the principality. We will look into the district of Rhos, which has been as mightily moved as any other district in Glamorganshire. We find that some signs of an awakening occurred as far back as June 1904, at anniversary services in a church at Ponciau. One of the special preachers had been to South Wales two months before and had come in contact with two of the ministers who entered into the Spirit-filled life in August 1903. He returned to his northern home with his heart deeply moved and was fully persuaded that the experimental knowledge of the fullness of the Holy Spirit would usher in a "new era in the history of the Welsh ministry."

The following Sunday will long be remembered in their church as their day of Pentecost. At the Sabbath morning service, the pastor asked for people to share their testimony instead of preaching his usual sermon, and a big sturdy man in the congregation rose and asked the minister if he would baptize him there and then on his profession of faith in Christ and if he would he do it without doubting. The whole congregation was moved, and, to the music of his mother's prayer, the young man was baptized, shouting, "Praise God for the privilege of following Jesus before the day of Pentecost is passed!"

Another from the crowd followed this one, and an after-meeting was held, when a young man who was the black sheep of his family was seen on his knees in tears; while two young men in the choir, old friends of his, offered up praise and prayer, mingled with joyous tears. His father, who was also present, shouted for joy and thanked God that the gospel had done what he and his wife had failed to do! The whole congregation was sobbing aloud.

At night, the service was so extraordinary that the people lost all consciousness of time and place, the minister lost his sermon, and, relying upon the Spirit, he was used in a remarkable manner. From this time on, prayer meetings were held every night in July, and the church was ready for the tidal wave that was to burst over the land in November.

The Channels in Northern Wales

Rhos

In November 1904, some churches at Rhos invited a minister from South Wales—one who had entered the Spirit-filled life in August 1903—to help them conduct special services. In giving the account of the extraordinary movement in Rhos, a correspondent of the *Liverpool Daily Post* said:

> If I had been asked a month ago whether a revival was probable in Wales, I should have answered No. It seemed to me that the higher criticism had wrecked the ordinary machinery of a revival, and that until theology had been reshaped... nothing could be done to disturb the prevailing apathy. But oddly enough, the revivalist [Rev. R. B. Jones] is one who, according to his own story, was at one time deeply interested in the higher criticism, and preached the "new theology." He felt, however, emptiness and coldness in his sermons. Attendance at a convention held in Llandrindod led to a crisis in his life. He felt himself to be a new man, and since then the writings of the higher critics have lost their attraction for him.

The services at Rhos began on the very day that the Spirit of God broke out in Loughor through the ministry of Mr. Evan Roberts! They were held in the largest church, the churches unitedly giving up their ordinary services for a time. The first week's meetings were devoted to the professing Christians, leading them to remove all hindrances in their lives, to fully surrender themselves to Christ, and to receive the Holy Spirit. At the close of the week, Christian workers stood confessing their powerlessness and others their lack of assurance of salvation. Seventy other professing Christians rose and walked to the vestry, in token of their full surrender to Christ.

After this, the floodgates of heaven were opened, and the Spirit was poured out mightily. The congregations grew and grew, until places of worship were unable to accommodate them. Thousands were eager to take part in the meetings. The revival had come! Four weeks after the missioner had left, a Wrexham paper said that "the whole district is in the grip of an extraordinary spiritual force which showed no sign of relaxing its hold!" The meetings were carried on by the people themselves, although the ministers were present. Some meetings went on from ten in the morning until six in the evening. From the lips of the humblest and lowliest people poured forth passionate appeals in prayer, which quickened the whole being. Men and women continually rose, often more than one at a time, to pray with a fervor that was inspiring. In the street, in the train, in the car, even in the bars—this strange power upon the town was, in hushed and reverential tones, the theme of conversation.

In the evenings, there were great processions, joined in by all classes, marching through the town singing hymns and occasionally stopping for prayer. The place was visited by great numbers of visitors, and prayer meetings were held three times a day, attracting many crowds. And souls came forward to Christ at every meeting.

A minister wrote at the end of March 1905 that the general result has been that the churches are on a far higher keel and in a spiritual atmosphere. He said that prizefighters and the biggest drunkards of the place were among the converts, and many of the most useful church workers were lifted from the very depths of degradation, and also that large bands of workers were now filled with the Savior's passion for souls.

The vicar of Rhos has thrown himself, heart and soul, into the work, and the Welsh church at Rhos has been the scene of a unique revival prayer meeting. Every Free Church minister of the district was present, and the building was full to overflowing. The vicar said he had attended many meetings but never felt such a thrill of emotion as he did on this occasion; the walls and hedges of disunion had been broken down; they were now fully united and knew no distinction! The Baptist minister opened with prayer, and the Welsh Calvinistic Methodist minister closed the service.

Bangor

At Bangor, the Spirit of God broke out in November 1904 in one of the lowest and poorest parts of the city. Theological students have been at work there, led by a young Baptist student named Morgan Jones, who had been in the South Wales district, where the revival was at its height. In the afternoon, the ministerial students from the Baptist and Congregational colleges met together for prayer and had wondrous times; and then at night, they proceeded to Kyffin Square—the "Whitechapel" of the Cathedral City. The Spirit of God has so worked in this spot, in a little schoolhouse, that it was said that all the poor inhabitants would be saved in a short time, and the character of the locality changed. The work of the Spirit in this poor center has stirred the churches of the town, and the people who sat in darkness have become the light to lighten the professing people of God.

In February 1905, special services were held in Bangor by another minister of South Wales who knew the Spirit-filled life. Large numbers of professing Christians were brought to full surrender and found for the first time in full assurance of salvation. The missioner found many of the theological students and others at the university manifestly filled with the Spirit of God. A consecration meeting was held after the close of one of the public meetings, commencing about 10:30 PM and lasting until 2:30 AM. About eighty believers were present when the Spirit of God fell on everyone with overwhelming power.

It is at Bangor University that we hear of a prayer meeting that took place in a smoking room, which arose through the humming of the familiar Welsh tune "Aberystwyth." The students present broke out into fervent singing, and all fell on their knees. Others came whistling or shouting to the room, and upon opening the door, they saw the sight and either fled or knelt among their comrades.

Carnarvonshire

In Carnarvonshire (also Caernarfonshire), the movement of the Spirit appears to have been first manifested at Bethesda, the scene of the historical Penrhyn strike, which produced social, domestic, and religious disunion.[5]

The S. W. Daily News reported,

The records of the police courts showed how families were divided, lifelong friendships were shattered, and so bitter was the feeling generated that in a large number of cases men would not worship together. Scenes sometimes occurred on the most solemn occasions, and those qualified to judge unanimously believed peace could not be restored during the present generation. But a week's "revival" services held by a Wesleyan minister (Rev. Hugh Hughes) were greatly used of God. Old friends have been reconciled. Members of churches have returned to pray by the side of those who had driven them forth. Women who had summoned each other go together to the daily prayer meeting, where five hundred women gather every afternoon. Members of the same family who have not spoken to each other for two years now meet happily together. The meetings last practically from 2:30 in

---

5. The Penrhyn Slate Quarry strikes (1900–1903) were led by employees who demanded better pay and safer working conditions.

the afternoon until midnight. Visitors from other districts attend and carry back the blessing.

Nantlle Vale

At Nantlle Vale, in the south of the county, prayer meetings were started voluntarily by the young people. Other villages followed the example, so that by the middle of December, practically the whole county might be said to be one great prayer meeting.

Holyhead

Reverend R. B. Jones visited the Isle of Anglesey in January 1905 and conducted meetings at Holyhead. Again, he dealt first with the Christians, and then with those who were brought into harmony with God, seeing the Spirit of God fall upon the unsaved in converting power. The Holy Spirit worked mightily, and the services became a veritable Pentecost. One deacon confessed that he had received the baptism of the Spirit, which he had sought for ten years. About forty went to the vestry, surrendering fully to Christ and receiving the Holy Spirit. Many were quite prostrated by the intense presence of the Lord. At the close of the week, on the Sabbath morning, every single soul confessed a complete consecration to the risen Lord, and some who were unsaved found the Savior. The closing testimony meeting showed that the entire church had been lifted into a new atmosphere, and many had realized their "Pentecost." God had worked marvelously in just one week, and the church was a "new" church. The pastor shared with his own people that he had entered into the experience of Galatians 2:20, so that the life of Christ might be manifested through him:

> I have been crucified with Christ; yet I live; and yet no longer I, but Christ liveth in me: and that life which I now live in the flesh I live in faith, the faith which is in the Son of God, who loved me, and gave himself up for me.

Llanerchymedd

In town Llanerchymedd, the missioner held only three days' meetings of the united churches. Again, he dealt with the Christians, his message on the holiness of God. On the first evening, sixty-seven souls were brought to Christ, and on the second night, remarkable scenes took place. The missioner, looking from the pulpit, saw a college student lying on the floor of the "big pew." Suddenly, the young man arose, and putting his hand in his pocket, he took out his pipe and publicly handed it to the missioner. Another student was on his knees groaning aloud and crying, "Oh God, give me strength; will I have strength to do it?" Finally, he, too, arose and took out his pipe and his pouch from his pocket and threw them on to the pulpit desk. Others followed, until the whole of the desk was covered with pipes and pouches of tobacco; yet the missioner had said no word about these things but simply proclaimed the holiness of God, which demanded a holy life on the part of those He owned.

While these scenes were occurring, the news was noised abroad, and people outside flocked in from their homes and even from the bars. Until right up to 12:45 in the morning, souls poured in to give themselves to God; no less than one hundred eleven converts were gathered in at this one meeting.

At a consecration meeting on Saturday morning, two hundred came forward to surrender themselves to God and to receive the Holy Spirit, after being taught what it meant. Again, the Spirit of God descended in power, for while they were on their knees in full surrender, the Spirit fell upon them, and all broke out in audible prayer at the same time.

Amlwch

In Amlwch, three days of meetings for the united churches were held, and the message that was preached was again on Isaiah 6, and the people were manifestly convicted by the Holy Spirit. When the messenger came to the "live coal from off the altar"—the cleansing fire from the place where the blood was shed, Calvary—suddenly, without one word of explanation, the Spirit so unveiled the truth that the majority of the large congregation of twelve hundred people simultaneously sprang to their feet, shouting, "Diolch Iddo!" ("Thanks be to

Him"), while the glory of the Lord shone so brightly upon the pulpit that the missioner fled to the vestry completely overwhelmed.

Cefn Mawr

At Cefn Mawr, near Rhos, the churches unitedly held services in September 1904, but it does not appear that the Spirit of God broke out in any torrential power until February 1905, when a minister from South Wales visited the place. On the second night of the February services, the power of the Spirit became so intense that the missioner was scarcely able to speak at times. At one point, the whole congregation burst out into singing, and then for a whole hour, many gave testimony for the first time in their lives. The climax was reached on Friday of that same week, when sixty to eighty of them gave themselves wholly to Christ, completely surrendering and accepting the Holy Spirit. The colleges of Wales have also been greatly moved. At Bala College, Professor Edwards says that if he ever saw the subduing, melting, abasing, elevating effects of divine power among his students, he saw them now.

Space forbids our attempts to record the movement of the Holy Spirit in other parts of North Wales. We hear of three-week prayer meetings in Merionethshire in the middle of December. The people united in prayer all over the villages and valleys of the county, until, at the Christmas season, a young man came home from the holidays from Glamorganshire a changed man, praying for his old friends and telling of the Lord's mighty working, until scarcely an unconverted hearer remained all through the valleys.

Other messengers of God have been used by Him, some from South Wales, and others called out and equipped by Him for service in their own districts. We hear of a farmer's wife at Egryn, and a young quarryman, as well as numbers of university students.

Reverend Elvet Lewis said, "I am more than ever convinced that 'the half will never be told.' It is a continual surprise even to those who know the land and the people intimately. There may be a few remote places still untouched, but I have failed to hear of one."

SEVEN

A MESSAGE TO
THE CHURCH

"He that believeth on me...out of his belly
shall flow rivers of living water."
—John 7:38

As we review the story in the preceding pages, the Pentecostal character of the awakening in Wales is unmistakably clear, and we are encouraged to believe that the wider fulfillment of Joel's prophecy is at hand. Undoubtedly, we are in a new era of the world's history, when we may expect to see supernatural workings of God that have not been known since the days of the primitive church.

The Question at Hand

Dr. Cynddylan Jones points to the question that is at the forefront today: *"Did ye receive the Holy Ghost when ye believed?"* (Acts 19:2). It was a question that rang out in the church of God during the awakening in Wales, and will continue to ring, having tremendous consequences on the world outside of Wales, should the people of God truly face it.

It is the call of the church, at the close of the dispensation, to arise and receive the Pentecostal clothing of the Spirit, which is her birthright, and her need for effectual witness to Christ in the world. What God has done for Wales is an object lesson of what He is prepared to do for His people in every land, if they will seek His face and obey the conditions for His Pentecostal working. This does not mean that the Holy Spirit will manifest Himself in exactly the same outward form as in Wales, as in sweeping in seventy thousand converts in two months everywhere; but, undoubtedly, if true members of Christ in every nation, including missionaries among the heathens—be they few or many—were each to receive what God means by a baptism of the Holy Spirit and fire, signs and wonders would follow in diverse workings, according to the circumstances and conditions of the various lands. It has been said that the world cannot be revived, for it is dead! A worldwide revival therefore means the quickening of the people of God into abundance of life. Were this to come about in every land, the *"overflowing stream"* (Isaiah 30:28) of the breath of God would quickly *"sift the nations"* (verse 28) and make its own channels everywhere.

But let us turn to Wales to shed light upon the laws that govern the Spirit's working, so that the children of God may intelligently know how to cooperate with Him for the fulfillment of His purposes.

The Object Lesson of Wales

The object lesson that stands out the clearest, and speaks the loudest, to the church of God, is the fact that the Spirit of God moved upon the unsaved in converting power as soon as the Christians in a particular church, or a specific meeting, were in harmony with God. The instances we have given emphasize this lesson. We see how in one church after two weeks of prayer, the Spirit dealt secretly with the professing Christians (as they afterward testified), and as soon as all were right with God, the Spirit fell upon the public service, and large numbers of unsaved people spontaneously arose and pressed in to the inquiry room, without any invitation! In another church, we see that the Spirit of God could not work until the pastor obeyed Him and personally dealt with the hindrance among his officers, although to obey meant to him anguish of heart and many tears. We find also in the crowded meetings in various places how the revivalist was given by the Spirit of God sensitive knowledge of the hindrances to His working. How strange the "block" was and how cold the service, until the curious spirit, the unreal spirit, and the contentious, or unforgiving, spirit were removed; and how quickly these departed when confession was made, or prayer was poured out to God; and how mightily the Holy Spirit at once fell upon the people and souls yielded to Christ. Again, in the work in North Wales, we see how whole districts were stirred after the Christians were brought into full surrender to God, and, upon entering the Spirit-filled life, were knit in perfect unity and fellowship with one another. Evan Roberts' prayer "Bend the church and save the world" is truly the message for today.

In past years, God has been using great leaders, special instruments called out and led into close fellowship with Him, to receive His messages for the people, just as He used Elijah, Isaiah, Daniel, and many others; but it was not so at Pentecost. Then, for the first time, God brought a company of people so into union with Himself, and one another, that He could speak through, and flow out of, a number of souls as *one*. And on the day of Pentecost, the Lord's ideal—"*that they may all be one; even as thou, Father, art in me, and I in thee*" (John 17:21)—began to be fulfilled and shown to the world. At Pentecost, the Spirit of God broke out upon the multitude, through a *united company* of people, all prepared by heartfelt, prolonged prayer—nothing unites like prayer—and yielded wholly to Him.

The object lesson of Wales shows that God works in the world when His people are right with Him. In brief, the members of Christ must be brought by the Spirit into full union with the risen Head and with one another—"*in one Spirit were we all baptized into one body*" (1 Corinthians 12:13)—so that the Spirit of life may pour out into the world. In the darkest, loneliest, farthest corners of the earth, the most isolated child of God may share in the worldwide blessing, as the life-currents from Him who is Life eternal circulate freely throughout the body of Christ, and overflow in exuberance of life on to the world lying in the shadow of death.

Again we learn in Wales from this same object lesson the meaning of *atmosphere*—a surcharged atmosphere. How mightily the Spirit works when the atmosphere is clear; how easy it is to speak and to pray when the Spirit fills the atmosphere! And this also is Pentecost, for in the upper room that day, the rushing mighty breath filled the house, together with the believers, who were then environed by the Spirit, as well as indwelt by Him. It is this characteristic of the clothing or environing or covering of the Spirit that distinguishes the Pentecostal experience from the Easter day blessing of "receiving the Holy Spirit." (See John 20:22.) In other words, the Spirit *upon* for service, as the Spirit *within* for life. Souls thus environed in God carry with them, so to speak, their own "atmosphere," and quickly know an atmosphere wherein the Spirit is hindered or grieved. We have thought much of changed people, but how little have we understood the power of a *changed atmosphere* wherein the Holy Spirit may freely work. "There was no result in individual blessing, but a changed atmosphere" may be said after a convention—yet this is the supreme thing after all, for in the cleansed and cleared atmosphere, the Holy Spirit is able to work out His fullest purposes in souls.

We see, too, in Wales, the attractive power and the all-sufficiency of the gospel to meet the needs of men. No "means of attraction" are necessary when the Holy Spirit fills and presides over the church. And if these things are so, some will say, "This awakening in Wales should shake the world!" Yes, and it will shake the world within the limitations we see following the first Pentecost. If we carefully read the story in the Scriptures, we find first 3,000, then 5,000, then "*multitudes both of men and women*" (Acts 5:14) added to the first few who met in the upper room. The Spirit-filled company grew, and the Holy Spirit presided over them in such intense reality that any sin was at once dealt with, so that great fear came upon the church and the people, as they realized the holiness of the God in their midst. The witnessing church filled Jerusalem with the sound of their message, but by no means did all Jerusalem receive it! Many were unwilling to yield and unprepared to let God have His way and upset their traditions. The tidal wave broke out in Jerusalem and at once swept in all who would yield; but the plan was that it must flow out to the world beyond. That it could not do so without Spirit-filled souls is shown in that the Lord had to permit a persecution to scatter His "channels" far and wide; and as they went, the rivers flowed on to the nations.

This is a pattern for us as we look at Wales today. The Spirit of God has swept through the principality and gathered many into the kingdom—yet by no means has all of Wales yielded to the Lord! The day of visitation will end, and the mighty tide will pass on, as it passed in a comparatively short time from Jerusalem, leaving behind members of the church to give their witness and continue the work of the Lord.

In closing, we cannot too earnestly urge upon the people of God the solemnity of this present visitation—we cannot hear about it, or come in contact with it, without it affecting our spiritual lives. God has shown to His people that He can work in the same way that He did at Pentecost as in an unbelieving age. Will His people heed the lesson? Or will they turn away and say, "Oh, yes, in Wales, but not here!"

The Place of Calvary in the Awakening

As we look to Wales, we also see the place the Holy Spirit gives to Calvary, and we may be perfectly sure that no overflowing stream of life will come when the people of God are not in agreement with Him in His estimation of the death of His Son. As we recall the conditions preceding the first Pentecost, we cannot forget that Calvary was a terrible fact to each person of the little company in the upper room. There is no Pentecost without a preceding Calvary. The fire that touched Isaiah came from off the altar—Calvary. The fire that fell in answer to Elijah's cry came on the sacrifice on the altar—Calvary!

John S. Calhoun wrote of the revival in Wales in *The Advance*: "Today there is one Hill more effectually in sight than Snowdon itself—a Hill 'without a city wall.' And as that Hill comes more and more into sight, crowned with its redeeming Cross, at times what burst of song, at times what hush of awe!"

Reverend H. Elvet Lewis wrote about the work in Wales in *The British Weekly*:

"What seems to me to lie at the heart…is the unveiling of the Cross."

"Unchanging Love, as it shone and shines from the throbbing mysteries of the Cross."

"The Cross stood unveiled, and thousands looked."

"Men and women smitten with the grief and triumph of Calvary rise to the labor and gladness of holier life."

Yes, the church is "bent" by the revelation of Calvary, and the Holy Spirit in Pentecostal power bears witness to the cross. Nothing but the supernatural working of God could have broken men at the feet of the Lord in the very city where He was crucified as an apparent criminal! And today, while men discuss theories of the atonement, the supernatural witness from heaven is no less needed, and, blessed be God, has now been given. The world has seen before its eyes that the preaching of the cross is in very truth the dynamic of the gospel and is the energy of God to actually and really save men from the bonds of sin. And what is of still greater consequence, the church of God has been rallied, as by a voice from heaven, to the banner of the cross. "We have been critics of the Bible when we should have been devotees. We have preached Christ as an ideal of sacrifice but have left out His atonement for sin," said a well-known minister at a conference in London; "Now, thank God, there is a return to the Book and to Calvary"; and another said, "The revival has brought us back to the cross of Christ."

A Call to the Church

The call at the close of the dispensation is now, "Church of God, awake!" Oh, may all be given anointed eyes to see the vision! The secret is open before the people of God. The Spirit flows out upon the world as the people of God are brought into harmony with Him. And the work in Wales shows us that He does not wait for the church as a whole to fall into line, but He will break out through single congregations, or specific gatherings, as they are brought into one accord with Him. In preparation for the rushing mighty breath upon the land, He deals, as we have seen, with pastors and people, lifting whole congregations into a spiritual sphere and bringing large numbers of church members of all ages into the Spirit-filled life.

May God go on to work deeply, until, in the day of His power, the whole church of God in Wales bears the marks of Pentecost, and the overflowing stream of the life of God flows on and on throughout the world, wheresoever it can find channels. These may be channels of individual souls asking for the baptism of fire and refusing to account the earnest of the Spirit that they have received in "Easter Day blessing" as being the clothing from on high given at Pentecost. And they may be channels of churches, or groups of believers, seeking in one accord the outpoured Spirit as given to the company in the upper room in Jerusalem.

Let me ask my reader personally, "Have *you* received your Pentecost?" Is it true of you that out of the depths of your life, God is pouring torrents of living water? If you answer, "I have sought, but no change has come," I would ask, "Is Calvary real to you?" Calvary, in its full-orbed meaning, is Christ crucified for you, and you crucified with Christ! Again, we would repeat, there is no Pentecost in spiritual experience without a preceding Calvary. We have not known our Pentecost because we have not known the full meaning of Calvary. We parted with our sins as the Spirit unveiled Christ dying for us, but we have kept *ourselves*, and hence made no room for the Holy Spirit. We may "repent," confess Christ, and seek to obey the Holy Spirit; yea, ask in faith and believe we receive; but if we leave out the crucial condition of the cross, which is the meaning of Peter's words "*be baptized*" (Acts 2:38), as interpreted in the apostle Paul's letter to the Romans: "*Are ye ignorant that all we who were baptized into Christ Jesus were baptized into his death?*" (Romans 6:3), we may know some measure of the Holy Spirit possessing our life but not the torrential power of Pentecost which the Lord foreshadowed when He stood and cried, saying, *"Out of his belly shall flow rivers of living water"* (John 7:38).

And how may this be? Jesus said, *"In [the day of Pentecost] ye shall know that I am in my Father, and ye in me, and I in you"* (John 14:20). Oh soul, yield yourself wholly to God in a faith that will not keep you back from Him; and the eternal Spirit will plant you into the death of Christ, and out of the depths—the deep springs of your inner life—will flow rivers, rivers, ankle deep, knee deep, loin deep; yea, even *"waters to swim in"* (Ezekiel 47:5), which will bear you and submerge you, as they sweep on and on and on; and *"every thing shall live whithersoever the river cometh"* (Ezekiel 47:9).

And he shewed me a river of water of life, bright as crystal, proceeding out of the throne of God and of the Lamb.

(Revelation 22:1)

The hidden springs of the awakening in Wales lie deep in the heart of God, thence breaking out to a dying world through the cross of Calvary—O wondrous cross!

> On the mount of crucifixion,
> Fountains opened deep and wide;
> Through the floodgates of God's mercy
> Flowed a vast and gracious tide.
> Grace and love, like mighty rivers,
> Poured incessant from above,
> And Heav'n's peace and perfect justice
> Kissed a guilty world in love.[6]

---

6. William Rees, "Here Is Love."

ABOUT THE AUTHOR

Jessie Penn-Lewis (1861–1927) was an evangelist and author from England. Evan Roberts, who was instrumental in the Welsh revival in the early 1900s, stayed with Mrs. Penn-Lewis and her husband, William, for a time. Mrs. Penn-Lewis had been an eyewitness to the revival. Her book *War on the Saints* (the updated edition is now titled *Secrets of Spiritual Warfare*), which Roberts contributed to, was written to counter what she perceived as the excesses of the revival and the deceptions of Satan at work to prevent the true work of God in awakening. It is still considered a textbook on spiritual warfare by many Christians. Mrs. Penn-Lewis also established and edited the periodical *The Overcomer*.